MW01167509

GO THE DISTANCE

Loveland, Colorado

Group resources really work!

This Group resource incorporates our R.E.A.L. approach to ministry. It reinforces a growing friendship with Jesus, encourages long-term learning, and results in life transformation, because it's:

Relational—Learner-to-learner interaction enhances learning and builds Christian friendships.

Experiential—What learners experience through discussion and action sticks with them up to 9 times longer than what they simply hear or read.

Applicable—The aim of Christian education is to equip learners to be both hearers and doers of God's Word.

Learner-based—Learners understand and retain more when the learning process takes into consideration how they learn best.

Go the Distance

Copyright © 2013 Group Publishing, Inc.

Visit our website | group.com

Editor: Bob D'Ambrosio
Contributors: Deborah L. Kocsis, Betty Stallings, Susan A. Waechter, Marlene Wilson
Art Director: Amy Taylor

ISBN 978-0-7644-9770-4

Printed in the United States of America.

10 9 8 7 6 5 4 3 2 1   18 17 16 15 14 13

Contents

Introduction **5**
> The importance of volunteer encouragement, accountability, and evaluation. How to build an energized volunteer-equipping system to go the distance.

1. Expectations **7**
> How to manage expectations in volunteer ministry—yours and those of your volunteers and church leaders.

2. Evaluating Your Ministry **29**
> Make sure your volunteer ministry stays on target and is effective by using these evaluation tips and techniques.

3. Accountability: Your Part in Preventing Problems **47**
> Help for solving most volunteer-related problems before they happen and four questions to ask when a problem does appear.

4. Accountability: Evaluating Volunteers **69**
> Discover how to make evaluations friendly, not frightening. Doing evaluations in a way that's helpful. Plus, how to handle challenging volunteers.

5. Encouragement Through Recognition **83**
> You're already encouraging volunteers through interviews, careful placement, and positive evaluations. Now add recognition to the mix, and delight your volunteers even more!

...Contents

6. The People-Energized Volunteer Ministry 103
An energized volunteer ministry is powered by people—both the church leadership and church membership. Here's how to involve people you need in a task force that gets things done.

7. The Prayer-Energized Volunteer Ministry 119
An energized volunteer ministry is powered by prayer, both personal and corporate. Here's how to plug your ministry into this power source.

8. The Goal- and Objective-Energized Volunteer Ministry ... 129
You're charged up and ready to move toward your vision. Here's how to take the next steps by creating goals and objectives.

9. The Change-Energized Volunteer Ministry 137
You're about to create some major changes in your church—and that can energize everyone involved. Or not. Here's how to gain permission to move ahead so your ministry thrives.

10. The Leadership-Energized Volunteer Ministry 147
A core team can take you just so far. It's time to put someone in charge...someone who'll keep the volunteer ministry energized and on task.

11. Wise Words and Encouragement—for You 157
We close this book with some wisdom, insights, and inspiration.

Sample Forms for Volunteer Leaders 165

Introduction

The importance of volunteer encouragement, accountability, and evaluation. How to build an energized volunteer-equipping system to go the distance.

Because you lead volunteers (or soon will be), we're guessing that you have been a volunteer yourself. In fact, you may be volunteering right now as you create or revitalize your church's volunteer ministry.

We volunteers know the secret: When we have a volunteer position we're prepared to do and we have all the materials and information we need to be successful in doing that job, it's *fun*. Not only do we *enjoy* serving, we *delight* in it. It's fulfilling and satisfying.

Each of the volunteers serving in your church deserves to have a delightful experience. And here's the good news: You can make it happen!

In this book, we'll focus on five pieces of the volunteer leadership jigsaw puzzle. They're pieces you'll fit together to create delightful experiences for your volunteers…

- **Expectations** often determine whether a person has a delightful, ho-hum, or poor volunteer experience. We'll look at how you can manage expectations in your volunteer ministry—your expectations and your volunteers' expectations, too.

- **Evaluation** happens when volunteers find out how they're doing. This doesn't have to be a challenging time—if anything, it's a time of celebration! When it's handled correctly, an evaluation is something volunteers actually *enjoy*.

- **Accountability** is expecting each person in the volunteer ministry to do what he or she agrees to do and do it on time and with excellence. Here's practical help with building accountability into your ministry and dealing with volunteers who are—and aren't—accountable.

- **Recognition** of volunteers may become your favorite part of working with volunteers! Here are dozens of ideas for shining the spotlight on volunteers, honoring their service, and helping them feel good about their involvement.

- **Encouragement** is like oxygen: Every volunteer needs it in abundance. We'll examine how you can create an atmosphere where encouragement is a natural part of your ministry culture.

We'll also discuss how to design your volunteer-equipping systems so they are energized to go the distance.

Energizing power. Solid leadership structure. Helping people embrace change. These ingredients will help you build an energized, thriving volunteer leadership process for years to come.

Expectations

How to manage expectations in your volunteer ministry—yours and those of your volunteers and leaders.

Expectations are our assumptions about the future—how we anticipate things will go.

In a perfect world, expectations are based on clear communication and agreements. But in the absence of those, people base their expectations on assumptions, implications, and wishful thinking. And that's a recipe for disappointment.

You see, what a person expects from a situation becomes that person's definition of what's reasonable and fair. And if others fail to meet those expectations, well, they're not being reasonable. Or fair. And they're certainly being a disappointment.

> Expectations are our assumptions about the future—how we anticipate things will go.

This principle operates *even if people never actually articulate their expectations*—to themselves or others! Expectations have the power to shade and interpret situations without ever making themselves known.

Here's an example…

Suppose you receive a letter saying you've won the grand prize in a contest you don't even remember entering. Your name was drawn out of a hat, and you're about to receive a check for a "substantial amount of money."

So you begin to plan what you'll do with the windfall. You'll give some to your church, some to your family, and with the rest maybe you can do some traveling. But where will you go? That depends on how large the check turns out to be. It's "substantial," but what does that mean?

Will you be able to book a vacation at Disneyland? Or better yet, Australia. And if you're in Australia, why not do it right with a two-week guided tour? And a stop-over in Hawaii to rest up, of course…

When the check finally arrives and you tear open the envelope, you find a thousand dollars and your heart sinks in disappointment. Substantial? They call *this* "substantial"?

> ## That's the power of expectations.

Had the check arrived without your knowing it was coming, you'd have been delighted. You would have celebrated because it far exceeded your expectations. You thought you'd only find bills in the day's mail; instead there was a *thousand dollars*!

But because of your high expectations, now the check you received seems like pocket change. It won't finance your dream vacation. It doesn't feel fair. That's the power of expectations.

And make no mistake about it: Both volunteers and volunteer leaders have expectations about volunteer roles.

The Importance of Clear Expectations

Since we're expecting something from our volunteer experiences, let's be clear about those expectations.

Here's where all your hard work will pay off. Because you have provided ministry descriptions and careful placement and you have helped set realistic expectations in the minds of your volunteers, they know exactly what they'll be doing. They know who they'll report to. They know how they'll be evaluated.

Of course, if you've not done those things…well, it's not too late to do them. Without the clarity that comes with ministry descriptions, interviews, and careful placement, you'll struggle with unclear expectations regularly.

Clear expectations help both volunteers and volunteer leaders have a realistic view of how the future will unfold, how tasks will be accomplished, and what the outcomes will be.

Before we move too far along, let's share a quick word about expectations and volunteers. There are two general expectations that have proven to be true again and again in working with volunteers.

- **Volunteers want to do their best.**

    It's rare to meet a person who signs up to help in a classroom or at the food pantry with the intention of doing less than excellent work. Volunteers sign on the dotted line with every intention of meeting and exceeding your expectations. Many things can get in the way of their delivering an excellent effort (we'll discuss a few later), but it's safe to assume the best about your volunteers and interact with them accordingly. Volunteers are typically enthused, inspired, and happy to be on the team.

- **When volunteers fail to meet our expectations, it's not always the volunteer's fault.**

    As leaders, sometimes the problem is with us. We have failed to provide adequate information. We have assumed something that isn't true. We have not defined clearly what we expect.

> If the problem lies with us, we can fix it.

If the problem lies with us, we can fix it. And if the problem lies with a volunteer, it's *also* our responsibility to proactively work to resolve it.

We may work directly with the volunteer or only with the person who supervises the volunteer, but we're likely to get involved. So let's talk about communicating clear expectations.

The Necessity of Clear Communication

You've probably already established many clear expectations for volunteers.

But there are still things you will need to explain—and have explained to you. Remember that volunteers are your *partners* in ministry; they have many valuable lessons to teach you, too. Communication is a two-way street.

> **Clear communication helps everyone win.**

Your ability to communicate clearly will help you in every aspect of handling expectations. Communicating clearly will help volunteers know what *you* expect. Your skills as a listener will help volunteers let you know what *they* expect. Clear communication helps everyone win.

Owning and integrating these three truths into your approach with people will help you manage expectations.

1. Everything you do communicates.

You can't *not* communicate. Even silence communicates something.

Here's an example…

Let's say you have a disagreement with a friend. Later you call and leave a message saying you'd like a return call so you can discuss the issue further and reach an agreement.

If several days pass and you haven't heard anything, you may call and leave another message. Then if a few more days pass without a return call, you may become angry or worried.

Is your friend ignoring you? Is your friend so angry he can't tolerate the idea of speaking with you? Is your friendship over? Or is your friend unable to phone back because he's ill? Should you call hospitals or phone a mutual friend who can confirm your friend is still alive?

Notice: *Your friend is communicating with you even though he hasn't said a thing.* His silence is speaking—but you don't know what it means and may very well assume the worst.

You're communicating all the time—like it or not.

> ## You're communicating all the time—like it or not.

You're communicating all the time—like it or not.

Interpersonal communication includes both content and emotion. The tone of your voice and your body language speak loudly about what's really being said. If your emotion and content are inconsistent, then the message is apt to be scrambled.

And for some reason, scrambled messages *always* take on the most sinister, negative meaning possible. It's a phenomenon that defies the law of averages, like dropping buttered pieces of toast (they always somehow land butter side down!).

For example, suppose you congratulate a volunteer on a job well done. You say "Great job!" as you hurry past the volunteer in the church hallway. You look preoccupied and distracted (you're rushing to a meeting, so your mind is partially elsewhere), and you don't make eye contact. You don't give the volunteer time to respond. You deliver a "hit and run" affirmation that's sincere but half-hearted. The result is a dual message: "I'm pleased—but not really."

Because your body language wasn't consistent with your words, the volunteer has to choose: Does she believe the words or the actions?

I'm willing to bet she'll believe the actions.

It's easy to forget that we communicate in so many ways...

- Through touch—a tap on the shoulder or hug, a pat on the back or handshake. They all have strong meaning to both sender and receiver. When you touch, touch carefully and appropriately.

- Through visible movement—pointing a finger, winking, smiling, scowling, folding our arms. These communicate volumes without using a word and often speak "louder" than the words we use.

- Through words and other audible symbols—including speaking, crying, and laughing, or a combination of these. Even a snort can imply that you don't agree with what has just been said to you.

- Through written symbols—in words, graphs, or even pictures. It's easy to be misunderstood when you send letters or e-mails, so be cautious. A rule of thumb: If what you need to communicate is corrective or confrontational, don't write it. Meet face to face, or at least talk voice to voice. Words are so easy to misunderstand.

2. Speak the truth in love.

In Ephesians 4:15 we read:

> Instead, speaking the truth in love, we will in all things grow up into him who is the Head, that is, Christ.

That biblical admonition requires that we be both truthful and loving at the same time. It's a hard balance to maintain.

When we strike this balance, we speak directly and clearly and get to the point. We don't gloss over issues. We don't adopt the conflict resolution strategy too many volunteer managers embrace: They *ignore* a problematic volunteer, hoping he or she will simply go away.

> "Straight, clear communication is exceedingly rare in the world."

Speaking the truth in love requires us to take into account the words, feelings, and body language of the other person in the conversation. We must be present and caring even if we're unhappy. There's no room for blasting a volunteer for a mistake or using sarcasm in any way, shape, or form.

Speaking the truth in love demands that we be clear about what we want—our expectations—and that we hear the expectations of others.

This sort of straight, clear communication is exceedingly rare in the world and, sadly, in the church. But it's healthy and helpful. It spares volunteers sleepless nights as they try to interpret what we want, hope for, or envision, based on our subtle insinuations.

When you speak the truth in love, so much can happen that's positive. It's worth learning this language of love.

3. Listening is communication, too.

Not sure who first observed this fact, but it's true. The world is full of good talkers but good listeners are so rare they're practically an endangered species.

It's been told the average talker speaks at a rate of about 175 words per minute, but the average listener can receive about 1,000 words per minute. Because of this tremendous gap, most people develop some very bad listening habits.

They let their attention drift to other things.

They assume they know where the talker is heading.

They use the time they're not paying attention to figure out how they'll respond—as soon as the talker stays quiet long enough to allow for a response.

But listening is more than just not talking.

It's like the story about a little boy who was in a music appreciation class. When he was asked to distinguish between *listening* and *hearing*, he replied, "Listening is wanting to hear." What a great definition! *That's* what listening is—"wanting to hear"!

> Listening is more than just not talking.

We all say we want to hear, but it's not uncommon for us to miss the vast majority of what people say to us. Don't believe me? Outline the sermon you heard when you were last in church. How much of what your pastor said have you retained?

The challenge for us as leaders in volunteer ministry is to train ourselves to listen deeply. To hear not only what's on the surface but also to hear what is *beneath* the surface.

> ## Our goal is to listen for the heart of what's being communicated.

Our goal is to listen for the heart of what's being communicated. This requires that we pay attention to the whole person. As Jim stands before us, we "hear" his life situation as he brings it to our relationship. We hear his actions, his body language, his subtle emotional cues, his voice quality, his voice volume, his eye contact patterns, his unconscious gestures. When they're all on our radar screen, then we're really listening.

We can do it—listening is a set of skills, not a rare gift that God has given to only an anointed few. I don't deny that listening is a complex process that can break down at any number of points, and if that happens, our expectations can get lost in the muddle. But the need to communicate clearly remains, and not just because it's the only way to be sure our expectations are being understood. It's also how we know that we are understanding the expectations of others.

And it's where we do ministry. Listening—heart-to-heart listening when we connect deeply with volunteers—is a gift to us both. When we move past discussing the weather to discussing how we feel about our faith or the illness of our parents or the pain we're feeling—that's ministry. We become open and truthful. We share who we really are.

> ## There's no shortcut when it comes to clear communication.

There's no shortcut when it comes to clear communication. And there's no set of skills you can use that will give you a better return for your effort!

Expectations About Quality

Just as volunteers want to do well in their volunteer roles, you, too, want the entire volunteer ministry to function well. We all want quality to be our hallmark.

But how do you get quality work from everyone in your ministry?

Here are some suggestions…

1. Communicate not just what work is to be done, but how it's to be done.

For instance, it's not enough for a volunteer to just show up on time to deliver a children's message. The volunteer must show up on time and be *prepared*, too. But what specifically makes a children's message a *quality* message? Is preparation enough…or is there more?

If leaders of volunteers are providing excellent orientation and training, your volunteers will have a clear understanding of what quality looks and sounds like. But that happens only if volunteers' supervisors are consistent and clear. Be sure volunteer supervisors do an excellent job with orientation and training!

- *Ask: "What do you need from me that you're not getting?"* Ask every volunteer this question every three to six months. It gets at whether the volunteer's supervisor has a leadership style that's connecting effectively.

   For instance, if Jane is a relatively "hands-off" supervisor and Shawn needs more guidance than Jane is providing, this question gives Shawn permission to ask for more help. This question also opens up discussions about training or materials that Shawn might feel he needs to be successful.

- *Ask: "What do you wish you knew about your volunteer role that you don't know now?"* Pose this question to each volunteer every three to six months, too. We want volunteers to feel comfortable in their positions. If they answer this question by telling us they're unsure how to handle classroom discipline or if they have a question about designing the church website, we know we've got a problem.

Until volunteers feel adequately trained, they're likely to feel fearful or uncertain. This question gets at what your volunteers feel about their training.

If you regularly ask open-ended questions that are designed to solicit evaluations and probe areas where you can improve the volunteer ministry, then you'll find out if there's a problem with quality *before* the program begins to suffer.

2. Identify the problem that's interfering with quality, and then set expectations for dealing with it.

Remember, your volunteers want to see high quality, too. They're not out to deliberately disappoint you or the people they serve.

In our experience, the following three most common reasons for poor quality efforts from volunteers aren't all the fault of the volunteers at all. If anything, they can be traced back to us as leaders.

- **A lack of aptitude**—At its core, this is usually the result of a volunteer being placed in the wrong position. Perhaps the placement interview didn't adequately reveal the volunteer's God-given abilities, skills, and passions. Maybe the volunteer didn't choose to reveal them in order to be placed in her current role—where she is failing.

  This situation needn't end a volunteer's service to the church. Instead, simply place the volunteer in a new role that's more appropriate. There's no shame in failing to thrive in a position that's not in line with one's abilities, skills, and passion for ministry, but the volunteer may feel embarrassed anyway. Communicate your willingness to reassign the volunteer, and offer support in the transition.

  Another alternative is to change the position so it fits the volunteer. Some positions are flexible enough to be easily adapted.

  Communicate to the volunteer your expectation that things can't remain as they are, that change is needed. Then, with the cooperation of the volunteer, facilitate change.

- **A lack of skill**—Picture a Sunday school teacher who loves children, loves teaching, and is ready and willing to lead a class every Sunday morning. Yet this individual lacks the skill that comes with experience. Leave him alone with the fourth-grade boys more than 20 minutes, and the room is reduced to charred rubble and chaos.

If there's aptitude but a lack of training, provide training. Use CDs and videos, provide books to read, identify workshops to attend. Even better, provide a mentor to come alongside the volunteer and help him grow in his skills.

If your best efforts to provide training still don't do the trick, look to redirect the volunteer to another role that's more in line with his or her current skills. This requires tact, but seldom is it a surprise when you tell a volunteer that things aren't working out. The volunteer already knows and wants to resolve the situation somehow. Remember, volunteers want to do well in their volunteer roles!

It's unfair to a volunteer to suggest that he or she is failing and yet be vague about the standards of excellence you require. "You're not good enough" is a message none of us like to hear. It's damaging, de-motivating, and seldom

> "Look to redirect the volunteer to another role."

true. What *is* true is that the Sunday school teacher in question isn't able to maintain classroom discipline and create a learning environment

Outline again what a well-disciplined classroom looks like, and help the volunteer see where there's room for growth. Jointly determine what will happen so the teacher can get the skills he needs. Then work the plan you've jointly agreed will do the job.

You've set fair expectations about quality because you've described what "quality" means in this context, and you've shown that it's possible to get there.

- **A lack of motivation**—Sometimes it seems that a volunteer just doesn't care. A teacher no longer prepares adequately, a committee member skips meetings without explanation, a church treasurer lets checks and bills stack up.

Don't assume that a change in behavior necessarily signals a character flaw or a total lack of concern. Rather than become offended, find out what the problem is, and deal with it. If the volunteer reports directly to you, find out if the issue is your leadership style. If that's the problem, you can work to change how you relate to the volunteer.

> "Find out what the problem is and deal with it."

A volunteer may seem less reliable if there's a problem in the ministry area in which the volunteer serves. The group may be experiencing conflict, which often de-motivates volunteers. If that's the situation, deal with it.

A personal or professional problem may be consuming the volunteer's attention, leaving little time or energy to fulfill the volunteer role. Find out if it's a temporary or long-term issue; if it's the former, offer a short-term leave of absence, and find out how you can support the volunteer through the crisis. If it's a longer-term concern, let the volunteer resign with your blessings rather than fade away.

And perhaps the volunteer just needs a reminder that what she does is important—and that others are counting on him or her.

> "Quality, like beauty, is in the eye of the beholder—until you define it."

Quality, like beauty, is in the eye of the beholder—until you define it. If an expectation of quality is church attendance a minimum of three times per month, then say so. If the expectation is that they create lesson outlines a week in advance, be specific. You can't hold volunteers accountable to unexpressed expectations. Until you clearly communicate what you want, you're unlikely to see it.

When you see a lack of quality that isn't responding to your proactive involvement as the volunteer supervisor, be prepared to act.

Your people matter, but so do the ministry roles they're in. If the quality of a ministry program is suffering because of a particular person who can't or won't make the necessary changes to improve, prayerfully consider how to redirect the volunteer to another position.

But first focus on what *you* may be contributing to the situation.

In his book *The Five-Star Church,* Alan Nelson puts it this way: "Assume that you are part of the blame whenever quality does not take place. Perhaps it was poor communication or training."

Good advice. He goes on to share the risk of stopping there without taking corrective action, "If you do nothing...team members who are responding well can resent the lack of equity."

> **Focus on what *you* may be contributing to the situation.**

Don't get caught in the blame game, trying to determine exactly whose fault it is that a volunteer is failing to deliver quality after you've set clear expectations. Act—so the problem doesn't continue as you sort out who's responsible for what.

It's *essential* to confront problem situations. The first time a deadline is missed or a volunteer fails to show up for a scheduled event, deal with it. Make sure the unmet expectation is understood by everyone involved. There may be valid reasons a commitment wasn't honored. But as a volunteer leader, you won't know until you raise the question.

And a word of caution: Don't try to "rescue" a failing volunteer by getting the staff (or other volunteers) to jump in and save the day. That action on your part sets an expectation, too, and may become standard procedure. You don't want to create that world, because you'll live in it.

Expectations aren't reality, but unless you are intentional about creating a culture where open, clear communication is what's normal, expectations may be as close to reality as anyone gets.

Attitudinal Blocks: When Your Expectations Aren't Met

Are you familiar with "attitudinal blocks"? Unfortunately, you probably are—and they can drain the fun out of running a volunteer ministry.

> **Think of attitudinal blocks as roadblocks.**

Think of attitudinal blocks as roadblocks on the way toward effective volunteer leadership. You're moving right along, expecting clear sailing, when suddenly you round a corner and smack straight into one. It can take your breath away and put you on the sidelines awhile.

You may never encounter the following four attitudinal blocks outlined here, but many leaders of volunteer ministries do. We bring them to your attention for two reasons: (1) You'll know you're not alone if you encounter them; and (2) we don't want them to derail you as you move ahead in your ministry. Unmet expectations can do that to you.

Don't think these problems are imaginary or far-fetched. The dramatic scenarios described below are based on actual situations. They are presented as dramas so you can use them as role-play exercises in a small group or in a workshop for volunteer leaders.

1. You expect as the volunteer ministry leader to be considered a full member of the team—but you aren't.

Actors: Volunteer ministry leader, senior pastor, assistant pastor, and secretary

Setting: Church office

Volunteer leader: I'd find it helpful if we could set up a weekly meeting to get together and exchange information and concerns.

Assistant pastor: That's hard to do, since we're all operating on different schedules.

Senior pastor: Our schedules are constantly shifting. There isn't a time during the week we're even all here at the same time.

Secretary: I feel a need for an information-exchange meeting, too. I get telephone calls and sometimes don't know information people want. Maybe if we all got together, it would help me to get more lead time on information and be able to "plug in" better.

Assistant pastor: But you already do a great job keeping ahead of things, and we both update you at least once a day.

Senior pastor: The church doesn't work like other organizations. We're always on call. We can't just set up a weekly meeting and always make it work. We've tried before, but it's impossible to maintain.

Volunteer leader: I understand it'll be a challenge, but I still want to set a time for a weekly staff meeting, if only to help me. I feel responsible for the information being shared with me regarding needs and how church members want to help. At our meeting we could discuss how to best meet the needs of all our programs and people and decide who would be best at dealing with them. I'd feel better if I knew we were following up effectively when someone wants to get involved in one of our ministries. I think we're letting lots of possible volunteers fall through the cracks.

Secretary: And I'd feel better if I knew everyone was being contacted. I feel bad whenever I type up the church directory and see names of people I haven't seen at church for a long time. Maybe they're being contacted, but if so, I don't hear about it.

Senior pastor: Well, I suppose we could *try* scheduling a standing meeting again and see how it works out. When do you suppose we could all meet?

They set a date, but the senior pastor then cancels because he later discovers he'd already booked that time for another meeting.

2. You expect to be welcomed by the pastor, but instead you're perceived as a threat.

Actors: Pastor, lay leader

Setting: Pastor's office

Lay leader: I've been meaning to ask you, Pastor, how is our new volunteer coordinator doing? She's been on board here six months and I'm curious as to how it's working out.

Pastor: *(Hesitantly)* Well…by and large, it's going very well. I mean she's very enthusiastic and a real achiever. She's getting things organized around here right and left! *(Pauses)* But sometimes I'm afraid she goes a little bit overboard.

Lay leader: How so?

Pastor: Well, sometimes she strays into my domain. I mean our roles are still pretty fuzzy about who's supposed to do what.

Lay leader: That could get frustrating for both of you, I'm sure. Give me a "for instance" and maybe I can help.

Pastor: Well…several times she's actually gotten into doing *ministry*… and that's what I'm here for!

Lay leader: What kind of ministry are you talking about? Can you give me an example?

Pastor: Last week when Mrs. Peterson died so suddenly, the family called her to go talk to the Petersons' teenage daughter—and that was while I was still helping get things straightened out at the hospital. Why didn't they let me know the girl needed help—instead of calling her? After all, *I'm* the pastor here!

Lay leader: It sounds like you're angry about that.

Pastor: Of course I'm not! I'm just…well, I guess I *am* angry. *I've* been called to be the pastor. What do you expect me to do—just sit here and let her take charge? Her job description says *she's* responsible to *me*.

Lay leader: You mean she's not communicating with you?

Pastor: Oh, she does that fine. It's just that she's supposed to find volunteers, plug them into programs, and run that show. *I'm* supposed to do ministry. That's my job.

Lay leader: So, it's when she starts caring for people that you get upset.

Pastor: I just don't want the congregation to get confused. Pretty soon they won't know where to turn—to her or me.

3. You expect current church leaders to enthusiastically embrace the volunteer ministry—and they don't.

Actors: Volunteer leader, secretary

Setting: Church office

Volunteer leader: Mary, do you have a minute? I've just got to talk to someone!

Secretary: Sure, come on in. The pastors are gone, and it's quiet for the moment. What's on your mind?

Volunteer leader: It's last night's council meeting. I'm so frustrated, I'm ready to quit!

Secretary: What happened?

Volunteer leader: It's not what happened—it's what didn't happen…again! I asked for time on the agenda to report on the results of the one-to-one interviews we've been conducting with church members the last two months. I wanted to remind the committee chairpersons to call the people I've referred to them.

Secretary: Sounds great. What happened at the meeting that upset you?

Volunteer leader: First of all, I ended up last on the agenda again—even after the purchase of a new garden hose! It was 10:30 p.m., and I could tell everyone just wanted to get out of there and go home, but I plunged ahead anyhow.

I asked four committee chairpersons how their follow-up calls were going, and not *one* of them had contacted one referral. Not one! Matt said he's been too busy. Amy says she hates hearing "no." Dave said it's easier to do things himself. And Roxie said she always feels like she's begging when she calls people.

Mary, these people *want* to help. They *want* to be called! Here these "pewsitters" everyone gripes about are finally volunteering for ministry, and no one calls them. It's ridiculous!

Secretary: I can see why you're upset!

4. You expect that you've got things under control, but you discover there's room for improvement.

Actors: Pastor, volunteer leader (who's been in that role for three years), and three members of the volunteer ministry task force (who've just returned from the Equipping Institute training they attended with the pastor and volunteer leader.)

Setting: Church office

Pastor: This is our first meeting since the training on equipping ministry. I hope everyone is still as enthused as I am about the planning we did at the training.

Task force member 1: I sure am!

Task force member 2: Can't wait to try out some of those new ideas!

Task force member 3: It was terrific to rethink where we're going with our ministry and what's really possible.

Volunteer leader: You know, when I got back, I realized we're already doing most of it—they just had fancier terms for stuff I've been doing for a long time.

Pastor: You've got some great things in place, but it's always a good idea to take a look now and then to see if we can improve on a good thing.

Task force member 1: For instance, we've never done personal interviews with our people—we've relied on time and talent sheets and casual conversations. My hunch is we really don't know a lot of our people. We need to do more discovery.

Volunteer leader: When you've worked with them as long as I have, you know them. I just haven't written it all down. But just ask me who is good at almost anything that needs doing and I can tell you in a minute. No sense making things more complicated than they have to be.

How to Solve Attitudinal Blocks

The fact is there's no simple solution for becoming a fully accepted member on a team that's closed. Or for changing the attitude of a threatened pastor. Or for convincing church leaders that volunteer equipping is valuable. Or, for that matter, overcoming resistance to change—our resistance or other people's resistance.

What all these situations have in common is that they are, at heart, "people problems," and they have to do with expectations. They defy a quick, simple formulaic answer that fits all situations. Each attitude is personal and flows out of someone's beliefs, experiences, and values.

You can't mandate that attitudes change; you can only seek to understand the people who hold those attitudes…and then work to change the attitudes by providing information and proven results.

When you're staring across a conference table at a row of disbelieving faces, it's hard to think the church board members will ever change their minds and will fund volunteer-equipping ministry.

But they will.

> You can't mandate that attitudes change; you can only seek to understand.

When you see your pastor shake his head and tell you—yet again—that there's no way he'll approve your interviewing each church member about their abilities, skills, and passions, it's hard to believe that his heart can change.

But it can.

You may be facing an uphill climb as you create an excellent, sustainable, thriving volunteer ministry. Maybe that's something you should have expected. To think something so valuable and precious could be birthed or taken to the next level without some childbirth pain isn't very realistic.

> "You are on a mission that requires faithfulness and tenacity."

So set your expectations accordingly. Determine you'll be in the process for the long haul. Called by God and given a vision of your church that means being doers of God's Word as well as hearers of God's Word, you are on a mission that requires two things: (1) *Faithfulness*—to hear God and do what he tells you to do; and (2) *tenacity*—the decision not to give up.

In his book *Servant Leadership,* Robert Greenleaf recounts a childhood story about a dogsled race in his hometown. Most of the boys in the race had big sleds and several dogs. Greenleaf (only 5 years old) had a small sled and one little dog. The course was one mile staked out on the lake.

As the race started, the more powerful contenders quickly left Greenleaf behind. In fact, he hardly looked like he was in the race at all.

All went well until, about halfway around, the team that was second started to pass the team then in the lead. They came too close, and the dogs got in a fight.

Pretty soon the other dog teams joined in, and little Greenleaf could see one big seething mass of kids, sleds, and dogs about half a mile away. So he gave them all wide berth and was the only one who finished the race...which made him the winner!

As Greenleaf reflects on the gargantuan problems we sometimes face, he refers to that scene from long ago. He concludes: "I draw the obvious moral. No matter how difficult the challenge or how impossible or hopeless the task may seem, if you are reasonably sure of your course—just keep going!"

And *that's* an expectation you can meet: never giving up.

> "If you are reasonably sure of your course— just keep going!"

Evaluating Your Ministry

Make sure your volunteer ministry stays on target and is effective by using these evaluation tips and techniques.

Some things just naturally go together—apple pie and ice cream, fish and water. I'd like to suggest another natural pair—planning and evaluation.

In the context of your volunteer ministry, there are two general sorts of evaluations that you will do:

1. Evaluating the ministry itself.

2. Evaluating volunteers who serve in the program.

We'll get into evaluating volunteers themselves later in this book, but for now, let's walk through evaluating your volunteer ministry. It's essential to do this, and it's something that many volunteer ministry leaders never take time to do at all, let alone do consistently every six months or year.

Evaluating Your Volunteer Ministry

You really can't evaluate your volunteer ministry unless you've done thorough planning. Planning and evaluation are tightly linked. You can't do a good job of evaluating your ministry or your volunteers unless you've developed a mission statement, planned how to implement it, and created ministry descriptions for volunteers. Have you done all of those things? Great, because *the better you plan, the easier it will be to do evaluations.* After all, evaluation is simply deciding if where you've gone is, in fact, where you intended to go—how well you have followed your plans and implemented your goals.

> Planning and evaluation are tightly linked.

You'll recall that in order for a *goal* to become an *objective*, it has to be specific, measurable, achievable, delegated, and move you toward fulfilling your mission statement. You probably struggled to create goals that fit all these criteria.

Well, it was worth the effort! Not only will those objectives you created help you do great ministry but they will make it easy to do evaluation. Because they're measurable, you can tell if you succeeded in doing what you set out to do.

> "Did you do what you said you'd do?"

Did you do what you said you'd do? Did you do it on time? Within budget? And if not, did you...

- fail to delegate responsibility to someone to achieve the objective?
- not allow enough time or money for it?
- let other, newer priorities change your overall goals for the year but forget to change your objectives and plans?

Remember, plans can change at any time. God may send you and your volunteer ministry off in a different direction, accomplishing your mission in a new way. That's God's privilege—but did you all agree that's what was happening? And did you change your action plans in writing?

Why Evaluation Matters

Many church leaders describe themselves as "people persons." You might put yourself in that category, too. That's why you're involved in a volunteer ministry—you enjoy people and love to help them grow.

So the idea of chaining yourself to a desk so you can crunch numbers and evaluate your ministry might seem like a waste of time. You'd rather be out helping volunteers be successful.

Understood—but it's still vitally important that you thoroughly evaluate your program on a regular basis. How else can you know if you're being effective and demonstrate to your church leadership that the ministry is worthy of ongoing support?

Embrace the idea of evaluating your ministry. It may not be the favorite part of your job now, but it will help you know how to better serve and support your volunteers.

Maybe you think you're already doing a thorough job of evaluating your ministry. Let's briefly test that theory. Take the following test and see what you learn…

Are You Already Effectively Evaluating Your Ministry?

Use these sample questions to help you determine if there's room for more effective evaluation in your volunteer ministry.

Rate each of the eight areas based on this scale:

5 = Always; 4 = Regularly; 3 = Sometimes; 2 = Rarely; 1 = Never

____ We formally evaluate our volunteer program, analyzing our progress on the goals and objectives we have set for ourselves, at least once per year.

____ We formally evaluate each volunteer to see whether he or she is accomplishing assigned tasks.

____ We talk with volunteers about their "ministry satisfaction," while listening carefully to their dreams, desires, wants, and needs regarding their work.

____ We provide an effective way for volunteers to give feedback to those people who are in charge.

___ We encourage volunteers to give feedback about how they perceive the quality of our ministry and the quality of their supervision.

___ When a new volunteer begins service, we hold orientation sessions.

___ When a volunteer leaves, we schedule and conduct an exit interview.

___ We contact a broad range of folks, within and outside of our program, to ask them to evaluate our effectiveness.

You have a possible score of 40 points. If you scored less than 35, you're missing significant opportunities to evaluate your program and volunteers and to benefit from the feedback.

Myths About Evaluation

Evaluation is a tool you use to determine if your program is doing what it's supposed to be doing. The evaluation process is as essential to the health of any ministry as is the planning process.

Yet, evaluation is the tool most often neglected by church groups. Why? Probably because many of us have mistaken notions about what evaluation is and does. Let's examine and put to rest some of those myths.

- **Myth 1: We're not perfect, so evaluations are only going to hurt us by displaying all our flaws.**

  Fact: Evaluations, to be valid, must highlight both "well-dones" and "opportunities for improvement."

  Example: At First Church, the people wanted to do a thorough evaluation of their volunteer-led food pantry. They braced themselves for lots of bad news about their budgeting, programming, personnel, and leadership, because the program had seemed to languish during the past winter.

Instead, they were pleasantly surprised by two facts that surfaced in the analysis: (1) A large new homeless shelter had been set up in a neighboring town, so that most of the hungry people in the area were now heading there for food and temporary lodging; (2) in spite of the new shelter, the church members discovered they'd been consistently feeding more people each year during the previous five years.

Their perceptions about the program had been flawed until the facts were uncovered.

- **Myth 2: Evaluations are purely statistical and boring.**

  Fact: Evaluations can be set up to record feelings, dreams, desires, visions, suggestions, and comments about what has happened—or what *should* happen. These can be more insightful and instructive than any statistics generated.

  Example: After the vacation Bible school program at Second Church, informal survey forms were distributed to the teachers, parents, and children. The forms (filled out without names) asked a few simple questions about what people liked, didn't like, and what they would suggest for improvement for the coming year.

  The statements were printed up and distributed for everyone to read under two categories: strengths and weaknesses. Surprisingly, this was a very powerful and poignant experience for everyone. The "strengths" comments were heartwarming and encouraging. The "weaknesses" suggestions, for the most part, were right on target. And plans were made for realistic change. Later, most participants said: "What a positive experience!"

- **Myth 3: Evaluation is something done by specialists.**

  Fact: Rarely do churches hire professional consultants. In fact, most churches aren't "mega-size," and therefore, consultancy is ruled out. Instead, all participants involved in a project or program are invited into the evaluation process by the current leadership.

Example: After Joe had spent six months leading the Men's Retreat Planning Team at Third Church, he was exhausted. Yet, because the retreat was such a success, he had a warm glow every time he thought about how his efforts contributed. Joe figured that glow was enough of a reward, so he was surprised when Pastor Smith set up an appointment with him and the rest of the committee members to evaluate how the process had gone for everybody. They all talked together informally. They also filled out a retreat planning feedback questionnaire to analyze during a second meeting.

Joe and his committee members knew they had the skills to plan and produce the retreat. Clearly, Pastor Smith thought they had the skills to evaluate it, as well.

- **Myth 4: Evaluation is an end in itself, a final report to wrap up a project.**

    Fact: Evaluations should help you decide what to add, drop, change, or keep. Program adjustment is the goal and chief benefit.

    Example: At Fourth Church, the children's pastor did a complete organizational development process, surveying all aspects of children's programming. He helped the participants develop a mission statement, set goals and objectives, analyze and gather resources, and put plans into action.

    A year later, when the evaluation process was completed, the leaders, volunteers, and parents decided to drop the high school "coffee shop" while adding a softball league for sixth through ninth graders. The evaluation process, in itself, was a tool for producing that change. Everyone knew there would be ongoing change and continual adjustment, because the new ministry configuration(s) would be evaluated annually.

Don't let believing these myths stop you from evaluating your ministry. They're myths—not accurate representations of evaluation or what it can offer you and your ministry.

Of all these myths, perhaps the one likeliest to stop volunteer ministry leaders from evaluating their programs (and volunteers) is the second myth: Evaluation is nothing more than stale, boring statistics.

Listen, it's important to do both objective *and* subjective evaluations to get an accurate picture of your ministry.

Consider the difference between the two…

> It's important to do both objective *and* subjective evaluations.

Objective Evaluation

This type is simple if you've planned well. Just review all of your objectives for the year, and determine whether your volunteer-equipping ministry accomplished what it set out to do—on time and within budget. If not, try to determine why. Then feed what you learn into next year's planning process.

The evaluation may reveal that you wrote a worthwhile objective but didn't allow enough time or didn't have the right person in charge. Or maybe you'll find that the need for a certain program no longer exists. Now you can drop or change that objective next year.

Subjective Evaluation

This type of evaluation is more difficult and rarely done in churches. Too bad, because a subjective evaluation is essential if you're going to be responsible for your people as well as your program.

You see, you've got to know whether your volunteers grew spiritually and as persons as a result of their involvement as volunteers. You need to know how they felt about the experience, whether their ideas were sought or ignored, and whether or not they received the support, training, and recognition they needed. And did they feel they were truly in ministry?

These aren't small questions, and they reveal important information.

Dietrich Bonhoeffer was a mid-twentieth-century theologian and a martyr to the Nazis. In his book *Life Together*, he suggested several questions any Christian community needs to ask to determine if the work it's doing is on target:

> Has the fellowship served to make the individual free, strong, and mature, or has it made him weak and dependent? Has it taken him by the hand for awhile in order that he may learn to walk by himself, or has it made him uneasy and unsure?

As a leader in your church's volunteer ministry, you need to know how participating in the ministry impacts people. Does it cause them to grow in their relationship with Jesus or become a distraction to their spiritual growth?

> "You are cooperating with the purposes and plans God has for his people."

You are involving Christians in ministry. You are helping your church do the work God has called it to do. You are cooperating with the purposes and plans God has for his people. It stands to reason, then, that the fruit of your efforts will be positive and good. But until you check through a thorough evaluation, you'll never know for certain.

The Three Big Questions

In my experience, there are three questions that must be part of your ministry evaluation:

1. What should we evaluate?
2. Who should do the evaluations?
3. What do we do with the evaluation results?

Let's examine these three questions in order…

1. *What* should we evaluate?

It seems obvious to say, but you need to decide what elements of your ministry you want to evaluate. That decision will determine what tools (such as surveys and individual interviews) you'll need so you can gather relevant information and do a helpful analysis.

If you've got solid goals and objectives in place, that's the place to start. They are designed to be specific, measurable standards that can be evaluated easily. For instance:

- Did you recruit and place 25 teenage mentors in nine months?

- Did you set up three new food distribution centers, with four volunteers regularly scheduled to oversee each one?

- Did you implement a teacher-training program and graduate five new Sunday school teachers in the past quarter?

If you accomplished your objectives, then you can go on to ask: *How well is it working?* If you were able to accomplish an objective but it burned out half of your volunteer staff to meet the deadline, there's a hidden problem. What looks like a success actually wasn't one—the cost was too high.

And if you *didn't* accomplish your objectives, you can ask: *What will we do about it—if anything?* Perhaps you could get those 25 teenage mentors if you recruit in two more high schools. Or maybe you want to abandon the mentoring program because you've discovered the liability insurance premiums for the program have doubled in price and you can no longer afford it.

It's challenging to evaluate a ministry. The elements of the program you choose to measure, the specific people you choose to interview— they all have a unique view of the program.

> It's challenging to evaluate a ministry.

It's important that you move past general impressions and get down to hard numbers and real statistics. It's not that "soft" questions—the ones that call for judgment from the people being interviewed—are worthless. They're valuable! In fact, you must ask some questions that get at the reputation of your volunteer ministry. Here are some "soft" questions you might want to ask...

Are volunteers enriching and extending paid staff efforts in achieving the purpose of the church, or are volunteers simply window dressing?

Is the money expended on the volunteer ministry reasonable and justifiable when cost per volunteer is computed?

Is the ministry accepted and supported by staff and administration? Do recipients of the ministry's efforts regard the ministry as valuable to them?

You can gain a world of insight by listening to the answers to these questions.

But you're also looking to discover quantifiable information. What can you measure and use as a yardstick from year to year to see if you're improving, static, or sliding backward in your effectiveness?

Find ways to measure the following items:

- **Time** is a resource given by your volunteers, both individually and in groups. Find out how many hours have been given per week or month, or whatever time period you're evaluating. Use simple record sheets such as sign-in and sign-out sheets, or have volunteers report monthly how many hours they've given to the ministry.

  Look for trends: Do you have more volunteers, but they're each giving fewer hours? Do you have some volunteers who give a great deal of time and some that you seldom see? Are there more volunteers in the winter than in the summer, and how might you use that information in planning?

- **Turnover rate** is a critical marker to track, too. How long does the typical volunteer stick with the ministry? Are there different turnover rates in different sorts of volunteer positions? If so, what does that tell you? What could you do to impact the average length of service among your volunteers? When volunteers consistently leave before the completion of their assignments or commitments, you've got a problem! Or when the average length of service remains only a few months, something needs changing.

- **Budget** is a major concern. Are you under budget? over? right on the money? Is there a predictable time of year when the budget is tight or loose? What factors impact that? Which parts of your program seem to be marginal when you consider the "bang for the buck" factor? What might that information imply?

- **Achieving goals** is perhaps the most obvious objective standard to check. Did you get things done you set out to do?

2. *Who* should do evaluations?

In the same way that it was important to have key "affected individuals" represented in the planning process, it's important to have them in the evaluation process, too. These people should have a say in how the evaluation is conducted and what is actually evaluated.

Affected people who should be represented in this process might include the volunteer manager, the volunteers, church staff, administration, and church members. All need to have the opportunity to evaluate the ministry from their perspective.

There are many tools that could be used to conduct the evaluation. However, because every volunteer ministry is unique, I strongly suggest that your core team draft its own evaluation tool.

Don't worry—you don't have to start from scratch! There are denominations and other church groups that have created evaluation tools. If you have a denominational affiliation, check with your office. But one downside of

> You don't have to start from scratch!

using a denominational tool is that they're generally very specific to a single denomination; those tools don't translate well for use in every church.

Let's outline the major issues you should include in your evaluation. Ask your core team to draft specific questions to fit under each heading.

Mission statement—Ask questions about whether the church or program mission statement is effective, reviewed regularly, or needs to be adjusted. Ask the same questions about your volunteer ministry.

Volunteer ministry descriptions—Ask questions about expectations and the clarity and awareness of written ministry descriptions.

Identifying and interviewing volunteers—Ask questions about how volunteers are identified and interviewed in terms of their abilities, skills, passion, personality, and desire to serve.

Matching volunteers and ministry positions—Ask questions about how volunteers' abilities, skills, and passions are connected to church ministry needs.

Recruiting volunteers—Ask questions about interviewing, describing positions, offering choices—the entire volunteer recruitment process. And include questions about marketing the volunteer program, too.

Training volunteers—Ask questions about how effectively you're providing orientation, education, retreats, and training courses.

Supporting volunteers—Ask questions about how your ministry is encouraging, recognizing, and offering support to all your constituencies.

Completing a volunteer ministry assignment—Ask questions about what happens when a volunteer ends a project or term of office.

Evaluating the volunteer ministry as a program in the church—Ask questions about how the entire volunteer ministry is functioning as a ministry area of the church. What's your reputation? How effectively are you involved? Are you thriving and energized to go the distance?

The person directing the ministry should constantly conduct an ongoing, informal assessment. Feedback from staff and volunteers, observations, comments at meetings, volunteer reports, statistics and records—these all provide a picture of the ministry's ongoing health.

But even if you are doing the job with such informal evaluations, please don't neglect periodic formal assessments! You'll find them useful as you prepare budgets and goals for the coming year. Use questionnaires and/or interviews with representatives from each of the groups affected by your volunteer ministry.

> Don't neglect periodic formal assessments!

The person who directs volunteers needs to become a real fan of doing ongoing evaluations. Why? Because in the course of those evaluations the volunteer leader is able to discover and correct problems before they become unmanageable. This assumes, of course, that leaders intend to act on the data and insights they gain from the evaluation process.

3. *What* do you do with evaluation results?

Keep in mind these four action steps:

- Disseminate

- Discuss

- Do something

- Don't file

In other words, *act on results.*

May we suggest you carve that one in stone? Hang it on your office door where you'll see it often—and so will those who work with you in the volunteer ministry.

You must act! Bring together representatives of all the groups involved in an evaluation, and talk about what you've discovered. *But don't stop there.* Keep bringing your group together for the consequent replanning and adjustment process.

This group will...

- Objectively examine the results.

- Explore alternative courses of action.

- Develop recommendations for improvement.

- Draw up a plan.

- Act on the plan.

A note: Don't forget all the good that's getting done! Be sure that in the course of discussion and planning, the strengths of the program are recognized, reinforced, and celebrated.

Evaluation not only enables but forces us to examine the quality and value of our programs. Yes, we certainly want to know how to do the thing we do more effectively. But that's not enough. Let's also ask the hard questions about *why* we do them and what happens as a result.

Exit Interviews

When you interview individuals who are leaving your program for some reason, it's not technically an evaluation of the volunteer ministry itself. But if you'll sift through exit interviews with an eye for trends, you'll get wonderful feedback about how your volunteer ministry is functioning. Exit interviews are used in many businesses because:

- The feedback about the organization is often direct and clear; the employee is leaving and therefore more likely to be candid with comments.

- Who is better able to provide accurate feedback than someone who is familiar with the company, its policies and procedures, and its management?

Your church isn't a company, but the benefits of exit interviews are transferable. Don't miss this opportunity to find out how your ministry is doing, where you can improve, and where you're doing wonderful work already.

> Set up the exit interview for *every* volunteer who leaves.

Set up the exit interview for *every* volunteer who leaves a position; don't reserve these interviews only for volunteers who leave while happy...or who are released from their positions. If you "cherry-pick" just people who are happy, you'll think everything is wonderful. If you consider only what disgruntled people say, you'll quickly become discouraged. Talk with everyone.

You might consider having someone other than yourself or the volunteer's supervisor conduct the interview. If there's a personality conflict, the volunteer might be more likely to reveal that information to someone else. You're looking for honest answers, so remove obstacles that might interfere with honesty.

Our friend Betty Stallings has developed an exit interview (provided on the next two pages) for volunteer organizations that you can easily adapt and use for your ministry.

Sample Volunteer Exit Survey Form

1. To what extent did you feel you reached the expectations listed in your position description? Share your reasons for any "gap" you perceive.

   _____

   _____

2. Was the time allowed to accomplish your volunteer work realistic? Explain your answer.

   _____

   _____

3. Did the church provide adequate orientation, training, supervision, and resources for you to accomplish your job? Comment, and offer suggestions for improvement.

   _____

   _____

4. What's been your greatest satisfaction?

   _____

   _____

5. What's been your greatest disappointment?

   _____

   _____

6. Were other volunteers and staff receptive and appreciative of your volunteer work? Explain your answer.

   _____

   _____

7. What were areas of growth in your volunteer role?

_____

_____

8. Overall, would you rank your performance as:

☐ Superior, exceeding expectations

☐ Excellent, you met expectations

☐ Needing improvement, you didn't meet expectations.

Explain why you chose that ranking.

_____

_____

9. What type of work and time commitment do you desire for next year? (Note: Only ask this if you would offer another position to the volunteer.)

_____

_____

Please share any other comments or suggestions.

_____

_____

_____

Accountability: Your Part in Preventing Problems

Help for solving most volunteer-related problems before they happen and four questions to ask when a problem does appear.

As you evaluate your ministry and your volunteers, you'll find opportunities to improve, to define problems, and then to do something to improve. That's the essence of accountability.

Nobody likes focusing solely on problems, but part of accountability is objectively examining problem areas and seeking to fix them. In these two chapters on accountability you'll see how that's done.

In this chapter we'll ask several important questions:

- Could the problem be the system?
- Could the problem be you?
- Could the problem be unresolved conflict?

Could the Problem Be the System?

Working with volunteers is almost always a happy, fun, and rewarding experience. If you've been involved for any length of time, you already know this! And to keep your volunteer leadership experience on this high level of fulfillment and success, one particular attitude is crucial: When a problem arises, it's best not to immediately assume that an individual is at fault.

> Working with volunteers is almost always a happy, fun, and rewarding experience.

That's right. Don't look to the individual volunteer first. Rather, look to the *system*—your policies and procedures, both official and unofficial.

We're hoping you're already assuming the best of your volunteers and nurturing respectful, positive relationships on your team. With those attitudes in place, you'll know that volunteers don't attempt to deliberately create difficulties; if anything, they go out of their way to *avoid* causing problems. When problems do arise, it's often the case that a change in the system or in the environment will bring everything back in line. You don't need a change in personnel.

But what, exactly, is a "systems problem"? A little story here might help you visualize the phenomenon.

Imagine a company that produces widgets. It has two manufacturing plants, Plant A and Plant B, and at each location there's a hierarchy of managers. Plant A produces the widget, and Plant B produces the packaging within which the widget will be shipped and displayed on store shelves.

All has been going well for years, until yesterday. Suddenly the packages are too small for the widgets! The vice president at Plant A picks up the phone and calls the vice president at Plant B. "What's going on with you guys over there?" he hollers. "The packages are too small! Here are the specifications we need..."

The conversation is brief; the crucial information is relayed. The packaging vice president then immediately calls his plant manager into the office. "What's wrong with you, Fred? The packages are too small. Check out these specifications!"

Fred hurries back to the plant and calls his foreman into the office. "Jake, are you nuts? You're really messing up here, and I'm not going to stand for it. Look, these packages are too small."

Jake runs from the office and hustles over to Phil's package-sizing machine and yells: "Phil, look at your calibrations! They're off by a country mile!"

Phil says: "But I thought Geraldo, the widget-sizing guy over in Plant A, was now making a new, smaller widget! Boy, I guess I was wrong about that—and sorry about the loss of millions of dollars."

At this point, Jake realizes he has several choices. He can assume there's a personnel problem and fire Phil for incompetence. Or he can go back and talk to his plant manager, who will talk to the vice president, who will call the other vice president over at Plant A. Then that vice president will talk to his plant manager, who will call his foreman, who will speak to Geraldo. And perhaps Geraldo will need to be fired, which should take care of the widget-sizing problem.

But Jake chooses a third alternative, a quick "system fix." He decides to install a phone next to Phil's machine so Phil can talk to Geraldo about the widget sizes he's been instructed to produce. In fact, now the two workers can talk about specs and calibrations any time they want.

And guess what? For as long as Phil has access to that phone, there is never again a packaging problem!

That's just one example of how a system solution can be just what the doctor ordered when a program problem arises. Adjust the system; solve the problem.

> **Adjust the system; solve the problem.**

There are countless possibilities for system problems, of course. So how could this type of thing occur in a church or other volunteer situation? Think about it…and test your creative problem-solving skills in a couple of possible scenarios.

- **Suppose…**

  Your Sunday school superintendent keeps forgetting to give you the attendance report after classes on Sunday mornings. Sometimes he lets you know as he passes you in the hall. At other times he calls later in the week and gives you a number. You, in turn, are either late or inaccurate in your reporting to the Christian education board. And you're getting pretty angry about that superintendent.

Your recommendations for a system change that could help...

_____

_____

_____

_____

(*A possible suggestion:* What if you both agreed to install a clipboard with attached pencil on the superintendent's wall? It could hold an attendance form ready for filling in, along with displaying your fax number, e-mail address, and phone number at the bottom of each page.)

- **Suppose...**

  Each day, after the kindergartners have their vacation Bible school snack time in the gym, there's at least one banana peel left on the floor. The custodian wants you to reprimand the teacher for being so incompetent.

  Your recommendations for a system change that could help...

  _____

  _____

  _____

  _____

  (*A possible suggestion:* Could you ask the teacher to stop serving bananas for snacks? Could the kids have their snacks outside? Or could a trash can be placed in the gym?)

Bottom line: Sometimes system problems are a quick fix, with few people involved. A few conversations, an update in your procedure manual, and it's over.

But sometimes they're at the heart of a large, far-reaching problem, and changing the system will require a significant amount of time and energy. Do it anyway—it's worth it.

When you sense that the system itself is your main problem, take these three actions:

1. Check the program evaluations you've done, and see whether there are any holes. (Look for steps you may be skipping in the volunteer leadership system outlined in this series or steps you aren't doing well.)

2. Set priorities along with actions steps for changing and improving the system. Make sure those priorities are communicated; you may not be the only one skipping steps!

3. Give yourself one to two years to do the fix or "plug the holes." Quick fixes are quick—but not always a fix. Take the time to do it right.

> Quick fixes are quick—but not always a fix.

Could the Problem Be You?

Maybe you don't need to focus your concerns on the system at all. Maybe it's just a matter of looking in the mirror.

When the problem is you, it's usually because you aren't taking care of you. That is, maybe you aren't adequately managing your own stress so you can more effectively manage the stresses among and within your volunteers. When leaders are stressed out and maxed out, ministries tend to experience more problems, and small wonder. The leaders don't have spiritual, emotional, and physical reserves deep enough to deal with issues that arise.

So consider your own life right now. Is it one of joy—or stress? Is it one that you'd like to maintain for a long period, or would you change it if you only knew how?

> Is your life one of joy—or stress?

How's your stress level?

Most of us who are involved in church leadership can relate to hectic situations like these:

- The alarm didn't go off, and you missed your 8:30 volunteer staff meeting.

- The senior pastor turned down that proposal you submitted three weeks ago.

- The church secretary was out sick, so you answered phones all day.

- You got stuck in a one-hour traffic jam on the way to a training session.

As the pressure mounts, so does your blood pressure, and soon your head aches or your stomach hurts, you begin snapping at everyone (including strangers), your heart pounds, and you find yourself either becoming more aggressive or withdrawing into yourself.

You're experiencing stress, and it's part of daily life for most of us. To be sure, a little stress isn't a problem. But when there's too much or we are overwhelmed by it, stress can take a hefty toll. Stress has been linked with most major health problems, including heart disease, hypertension, ulcers, and cancer.

> Like it or not, stress is no stranger in the church.

And like it or not, stress is no stranger in the church. As the leader of volunteers, you're responsible for the quality of work performed by people you don't pay and whom you may not directly supervise. That's stress!

You've got to learn to handle stress well for several reasons, not the least of which is that without mastering stress, you'll never last long in a ministry position. You'll feel the joy and fun drain from your ministry; it will become drudgery you'd rather avoid.

Plus, when you handle stress well, problem situations tend to gradually diminish—for reasons that have nothing to do with your volunteers or pastor.

Handling stress well can mean:

- **You don't overreact.** If you're overly stressed, you'll overreact to people and situations that appear to be problems. You'll treat small interruptions as major issues—because, in truth, the problem is you. You've got to understand and recognize when inner stress is fogging your vision and warping your assessment of others and the work they are doing.

- **You model stress-free volunteerism.** If you've learned how to recognize and manage your own stress levels, you can then model and teach those skills to your volunteers. It's amazing how many "problem people" can become ideal volunteers if their stresses are cared for. If they're nurtured and given hope, they can set about their tasks with renewed energy and positive spirits. It doesn't *always* work that way, of course. But isn't it worth trying to salvage those who, because of stress, are unhappy—and are making others unhappy?

Let's revisit those stressful scenarios listed on page 52. There are three stressful components in each of them:

The stressor—the event or incident in the environment that arouses stress.

Your perception of that stressor—which determines how it affects you.

Your reaction or physical and emotional response to the stressor, based on that perception—it's not the same for everybody.

This information explains why some people view a seemingly stressful incident calmly, while other people are running in circles, panicked and screaming.

Let's take the traffic jam, for instance. One person impatiently views it as an intrusion on his freedom of movement and a maddening inconvenience, while the person in the next car may regard it as a chance to listen to a favorite CD or unwind before reentering his or her life with the family. It's the same traffic jam—but the perceptions and reactions are very different. The traffic jam is stress-*inducing* to one driver and stress-*reducing* to another driver.

That unstressed driver is undoubtedly employing one of three stress-management strategies. They're the same options we all have when we feel the tension of stress building:

- Remove yourself from the situation or stressor;

- Reengineer the situation so it's no longer stressful; or

- Teach yourself to react differently regarding things you find stressful that you can't change or leave.

Prolonged, unrelieved stress is the most debilitating kind of stress, so work on taming those stressors first. Although you can list dozens of sources of stress in your life, probably very few of them are actually creating problems for you.

> **Most people handle the vast majority of potentially stressful situations successfully.**

Most people handle the vast majority of potentially stressful situations successfully. Appropriate stress is often what provides excitement and zest in our lives, and many days would be boring if all traces of stress disappeared.

But there are those long-term stressors that can do us damage. Equally damaging is responding to a small stressor as if it were a life-threatening, fire-breathing dragon attacking you.

Here are four questions that will help you determine if a stressor deserves a five-alarm response, or can just be identified and shrugged off:

- Is there really a legitimate threat in this situation?

- Is your interpretation of the event more of a threat than its actuality?

- Is the event really worth a fight?

- If you do decide to fight, will it make any difference?

Your goal is to learn to expend an appropriate amount of energy on problems or stressors, based on their long-term importance to you. If you overreact to small things (like traffic jams and lost socks), you'll use up your ability to handle stress on the small stuff. There will be no energy left to tackle the big stuff.

In your volunteer ministry you will undoubtedly be challenged—that comes with the territory. At times you'll be overworked. And you'll probably feel unappreciated now and then (we all do).

But you can be attentive to your own stress, health, and happiness—and make sure that when problems arise, your presence helps resolve them, not create them.

A seductive temptation for leaders is to try to be all things to all people (often referred to, appropriately enough for church volunteer ministry leaders, as the "Messiah complex"). It leads to longer and longer hours, more and more projects, weekend and evening commitments, and eventual burnout.

It often appears easier, quicker, and more effective to do things yourself rather than invest the time and effort to recruit, train, and supervise a team for effective ministry. Besides, it's kind of nice to feel you have climbed on that pedestal called

> The only direction for getting off of a pedestal is down.

"indispensable," right? But remember, the only direction for getting off of a pedestal is down, and it behooves you to climb down before you fall off.

You are *not* the Messiah! You are simply a person who works with and through others to accomplish ministry goals. And how those other people feel about working with you has…

tremendous impact on both the quality and quantity of work they'll do,

which has a great impact on your own perceptions of your effectiveness as a manager,

which has an awesome impact on both your own stress level and that of your subordinates,

which has a mind-boggling impact on your health and peace of mind,

which has a gargantuan impact on how many "problem volunteers" you are encountering (or creating?)—*and* how you deal with them.

If you're trying to do too much for too long, I can tell you this: When problems pop up in the ministry, one of the culprits will probably be you.

In her book *Survival Skills for Managers*, Marlene Wilson lists several suggestions to help manage the stress.

1. Clarify your value system so you're expending the greatest amount of time and energy on those things of greatest value to you.

2. Take good care of yourself physically through exercise and good nutrition.

3. Create and use personal support systems.

4. Learn to let go of past resentments, toxic relationships, and bad health habits.

5. Seek variety, and develop a well-rounded personality— avoid being a one-dimensional workaholic.

6. Maintain optimism, and keep some optimists around you.

7. Try to make the workplace and work itself more enjoyable.

8. Don't let small things become a hassle.

9. Take responsibility to change what needs to be changed.

10. Value and develop creativity and flexibility.

11. Have faith that things can be different.

Have we overstated the case about the importance of your personal stress management and honoring your limitations? Don't think so.

You see, most effective volunteer managers and leaders have been, first of all, effective as *persons*. By that we mean they are well-rounded, involved, enthusiastic lifelong learners who always see themselves on a "journey of becoming." As such, they're fully qualified to deal with people who are living out less than their potential and those who are "problems" because they're stressed, in the wrong job, or have determined to handle life's problems in ways that—sadly—irritate others!

We can only approach those folks with love and kindness when we have the emotional and spiritual energy to do so. Will we seek to redeem every problem situation and its participants for the good? Yes, but we'll also approach these persons with firmness and decisiveness.

Why? Because our volunteer ministry is at stake. Kingdom work must move forward.

Could the Problem Be Unresolved Conflict?

Any time we get serious about accountability, we'll run into conflict. That can be uncomfortable for Christ-followers because we figure that if we truly love one another—like the Bible says!—then interpersonal discord won't happen.

The result is that we become chronic avoiders and deniers. We let conflicts fester instead of dealing with them openly and well.

> We become chronic avoiders and deniers.

One of the most eye-opening discoveries that can be made about conflict is that there's a positive, productive side to it—and a positive, productive way to deal with it.

Consider...

- When in conflict, seek a resolution that everyone involved can accept. It's not always a "win-lose" situation. With creativity and resolve we can usually find a "win-win" solution.

- Remember that conflict produces lots of energy. We get fired up and passionate. Let's remember to use that energy for good, especially directing it toward problem solving.

- As you seek resolution, be sure you're digging down to the real issues, not just the on-the-surface presenting problems. It's easy to solve the wrong problems just so we can say we solved something.

- Keep in mind that conflict is neither good nor bad. It simply is.

- Make problem-solving your goal rather than trying to make everyone happy and friendly. Not everyone may emerge happy, but they can emerge heard and valued.

> **"Conflict is neither good nor bad."**

The first thing for us to accept is something that probably feels completely wrong: *Conflict is not bad.* It's not good, either. Conflict simply exists. It's the by-product of having so many of us crowded onto this planet, each of us with our own agendas, interests, goals, and values. We come into conflict because we're all here. About the only place you can pack people close together without conflict erupting is in a cemetery.

What's required is that we choose to not let conflict poison our relationships. Instead, we can let it be a powerful catalyst for significant change—perhaps change for the better.

Conflict itself isn't fun or painless. But it's not always bad, either, as demonstrated by how tough times, challenges, obstacles, and even affliction can prompt our spiritual growth. Consider this passage from the book of James:

> *Consider it pure joy, my brothers, whenever you face trials of many kinds, because you know that the testing of your faith develops perseverance. Perseverance must finish its work so that you may be mature and complete, not lacking anything.* (James 1:2-4)

When you encounter conflict—and you will—keep in mind that, if we choose:

Our trials can produce patience.

Our sufferings can produce mercy.

Our sicknesses can produce antibodies.

Our loneliness can produce compassion.

Our sadness can produce pity.

Our anger can produce righteous action for change.

May we suggest that when conflict arises, you choose to make your first response (after the initial shock or pain): "I wonder what new—and potentially wonderful—results this situation could produce?"

Conflict always generates great energy; your job is to direct and focus that energy toward problem-solving activity rather than toward people-destroying activity. Learning to make conflict constructive makes working with volunteers even more fun and rewarding.

It takes some effort to make conflict into something positive, of course. Two essential skills are needed: (1) To know when you're "stuck"—and how to get unstuck with certain conflict-diffusing techniques; and (2) to master four steps to reaching agreements.

The rest of this chapter will help equip you in both areas. While having conflict is neither good nor bad, letting conflict simmer and stew is most definitely *not* good.

When You Get Stuck

When conflicts arise, you need to seek a win-win solution—one where everyone involved is heard, understood, and emerges with something he or she needs.

The following techniques can help you get "unstuck" and move toward a win-win solution. These techniques will help defuse a conflict situation. Keep in mind they're just tools and temporary fixes, though—you don't want to slap an adhesive bandage on a broken bone and assume everything will heal up fine.

When you find yourself in conflict, invest the time to resolve it thoroughly.

- **Use "I" statements.**

  When you express feelings in a conflict situation, it's wise to use "I" statements rather than "you" statements. It's easier to avoid making accusations—or appearing to make accusations—when you're talking about your own feelings rather than the other person's feelings.

Confronting, even with the best of intentions and with heartfelt love and concern for the other person, is a volatile process. It's better to share

> ## Confronting is a volatile process.

what you know to be true (your feelings and motivations) rather than what you only assume to be true (the other person's feelings and motivations).

Here's an example of the difference in these approaches. You'll note that both comments refer to the same event.

At the church board meeting, there was a comment made about Frank. Now Frank is talking with the person who made the comment.

Using an "I" statement: *"I feel bad about something I heard in the meeting last night. I'd like to talk it over."* Notice that this sounds like a report, not an attack. Frank is owning his feelings.

Using a "you" statement: *"You said something hurtful last night. You need to deal with it."* This sounds like an accusation—an attack. The person Frank is confronting will likely grow defensive very quickly.

See the difference? Who would you rather talk about a problem or conflict with, someone using "I" statements or someone who is on the offensive?

Try turning these examples of confrontation into "I" statements:

"You never send out the agenda far enough in advance. You're not giving me time to prepare for our meetings."

_____

_____

_____

_____

(Here's one possible revision of the statement above: *"I've noticed that I'm receiving the agenda pretty close to our meeting times. But I'd like more time to prepare."*)

"Clearly, you don't care how I might be hurt by this."

_____

_____

_____

_____

"Some of us in this program think you're being insensitive about causing embarrassment."

_____

_____

_____

- **Use a "when–feel–please" formula when confronting others.**

  This is an excellent way to frame your statements when you have a (usually minor) grievance about someone's behavior that you need to raise—without starting a fight. It's direct, incorporates an "I" statement, and is specific about what can be done to remedy the situation. Your comment to the person with whom you have conflict combines these three elements. Here's how the three-part statement works:

  Identify when the issue arose: _"When you open the windows early in the morning..."_

  Identify a feeling: _"I begin to feel cold..."_

  Use the word _please: "So could you please wait until later in the day to do that?"_

  Here are some other examples:

  "When you come home late without warning, I feel neglected and unimportant. Honey, please give me a phone call when you know you're going to be late."

  "When you tell the guys at the gym about an upcoming church meeting, I feel left out of the loop. Could you please call or send me an e-mail, since I'm not a gym member?"

- **Avoid rhetorical questions.**

    Need I say more here? We all do it, so see if you recognize yourself in any of these questioning statements—whether they've been uttered at home, school, work, or church:

    "Why can't I depend on you?"

    "Why can't you see that you're putting people off?"

    "Wouldn't it be better if you just _____?"

    "Why can't you be more like your brother?"

    "Why do you say such things?"

    "Is this casserole too salty or what?"

    "Why can't you ever learn?"

    "Who said you could do that?"

> State your feelings, needs, and ideas directly.

    Most rhetorical attacks start with the question "Why," which is usually a clue that what follows will be worthless for increasing understanding and cooperation. "Why" is one of the least effective approaches to resolving conflict; questioning is a great way to fan flames of anger.

    Instead, state your feelings, needs, and ideas directly.

- **Leave all sarcasm behind—forever.**

    Humor in relationships is dangerous. A well-placed joke can work wonders in a tense situation, but joking can also backfire. It's often not worth the risk to make light of something that's potentially a sore subject between you and another person.

    Sound advice says you should avoid joking with volunteers. If you do choose to joke with a volunteer, be wise. Know who you're dealing with. Be sure what you're saying cannot be construed as offensive—and that's tough to do!

And here's the Golden Rule about sarcasm: Banish it. It's *never* worth the risk. It offers a multitude of opportunities for misinterpretation and hurt feelings. What you say may sound cute at the time, but it will come back to haunt you later.

Four Steps for Getting to an Agreement

There's no right or wrong way to reach agreements when people are in conflict. Whatever works…works! However, I'd like to summarize four basic steps that often produce an excellent chance of reaching good agreements.

1. Discover and emphasize what the participants hold in common.

You discover common ground by bringing people together and getting them sharing about "where they are." Ask everyone to respectfully take a turn speaking, and ask that everyone else respectfully listen without comment.

Your job is to note the areas, no matter how small, where people already agree. These are the places to begin building an even broader "island" of agreement. After sharing, highlight areas of agreement. Everyone may be surprised at the common ground already held!

2. Attempt to "unfreeze" stalemates.

During the sharing, you'll uncover specific places where conflicting parties are in an apparent deadlock. For instance, some volunteers want your training program to be held during morning hours. They are quite adamant about this because it fits with their home and school schedules.

Other participants demand an evening program that won't cut into their day jobs. In order to work at bringing the sides to some kind of resolution, you might try one or more of these approaches:

- **String it out.** Not every conflict can be solved in one sitting. Your first goal may be to get agreement that you'll meet several times to deal with the conflict.

- **Reduce the personal pain.** Explore what it is about a solution that causes the most pain for persons on either side of the issue. How can you eliminate or reduce some of that pain? For example, could you arrange for morning child care for those who need to be home until noon?

- **Suggest payoffs.** What will it take to get people to accept a less than ideal solution? Can you compensate or reward them in ways that make it worthwhile for them to rearrange their work schedules?

- **Create compromises.** Get both sides to agree to give in so that they can meet in the middle. For example, meet in the evening during the first month and in the morning during the second month.

- **Find a new alternative.** One side wants a morning program, and the other side wants an evening program. But what if instead of meeting as a group for instruction, you set up a system of one-on-one mentoring? Then pairs of individuals could meet together based on their own personal schedules.

> Creatively brainstorm solutions without setting limits.

The key: Creatively brainstorm solutions without setting limits. In the initial stages, everyone should know that no possible solution will be considered foolish or out of bounds. Let the possibilities be raised and "placed in the hopper" for future consideration. Creative thinking is the key.

3. Produce a written contract that outlines all specific agreements between the parties.

Make this summary as clear and as simple as possible. This can be as simple as e-mailing meeting minutes with a clear statement about how the conflict was resolved and how people agreed to proceed. Or it can be a more formal document that's filed in the church office, perhaps after everyone has signed it. Use your common sense about how elaborate you need to be, based on the gravity of the issues.

Don't generalize; be specific. And consider building in consequences everyone is aware of, should one or more persons break the agreement.

4. Schedule a follow-up meeting.

This meeting creates an opportunity for your evaluation process and guarantees that you won't come to agreements and then forget about them. It's human nature to slip back into old patterns of conflict unless we're diligent about monitoring our progress.

Accountability: Evaluating Volunteers

Discover how to make evaluations friendly, not frightening. Doing evaluations in a way that's helpful. Plus, how to handle challenging volunteers.

Uh-oh…a problem has arisen. You look at the system for solutions. You look to your own stress levels and check for burnout. Then you work toward constructive conflict resolution if there's a disagreement.

But suppose the root of the problem turns out to be a particular volunteer? And no matter how much you try to find a solution, every finger keeps pointing back to that one specific person?

"Problem volunteers" are rare, but they do exist. When it comes to evaluating a volunteer who's a problem, we urge you to embrace these two accountability principles that need to be applied to *all* volunteers:

> Problem volunteers are rare, but they do exist.

- **Never lower standards for volunteers.** It's the ultimate put-down for volunteers to feel that what they do is so unimportant, it doesn't matter if they do it well—or even at all.

- **View volunteers as unpaid staff, and always hold them accountable for their commitments and actions.** If it would matter if your paid pastor did it, it matters if a volunteer does it—or doesn't do it. Treat paid and unpaid staff the same.

If You Have a "Problem Volunteer"

If a volunteer is unable to function in his or her role, that's a problem... but he or she may *not* be a problem volunteer.

If you see that the problems generated by a volunteer far outweigh the good coming from his or her efforts or if that volunteer is intentionally making things difficult for everyone and therefore damaging your team or ministry, *that's* a problem volunteer.

So how do you handle that sort of person? Let's approach this issue in two ways: by being *proactive* and *reactive*.

We'll focus on proactively preventing problem-volunteer situations in the first place—by making sure we're conducting ongoing performance reviews. Being proactive is one way you can make certain you very seldom, if ever, see a problem volunteer.

Then we'll talk about being reactive—how to react when it's obvious that no solution other than separating a volunteer from your program will work to keep your ministry healthy.

Being Proactive

The great news is that you can prevent lots of problems in your volunteer ministry simply by being proactive with evaluations (also called performance reviews). After all, performance reviews have the potential to be overwhelmingly positive—and most are!

> "Think of performance evaluations as an *affirming* event."

I want to encourage you to think of performance evaluations as an *affirming* event, not one to be feared, ignored, or (as in some church settings) avoided. They're times we can celebrate what volunteers have accomplished and what a difference they're making in the church.

If you're focusing on the "well-dones" as well as the areas that could use improvement, you'll find your conversation well seasoned with words like *success, growth, affirmation, new opportunity,* and *mentor*.

When volunteers walk away from their evaluations, they should feel ten feet high, even if you've identified some things to work on. Why?

Because volunteers *want* to get better at what they do. They *appreciate* your taking the time to carefully observe them and suggest ways they can make an even bigger impact. Volunteers are *grateful* you notice and take them seriously. See why evaluations can be a fun time?

Betty Stallings, volunteer leadership consultant and author, helps us look at the review process in a nutshell, using four key concepts.[1]

1. Schedule reviews with regularity.

Successful performance reviews connect the person who assigns the work with the person who does it so the two can talk. It may seem obvious that this is a good idea, but it's amazing how many churches fail to schedule such periodic reviews, although the church can only benefit from such a move (see concept 2).

In the review meetings, volunteer and leader discuss what they expect from themselves and each other and how well those expectations are being met. Performance reviews should be nonthreatening, constructive, supportive, flexible, and empowering. The aim: to encourage volunteers to stretch for high standards and determine how the church can help the volunteer achieve his or her goals.

Performance reviews can be effective and renewing. But that won't happen automatically. Here are the essential elements for success:

- As they enter the organization, volunteers should be told of the feedback system, including the system of performance reviews.
- Be sure both the volunteer and supervisor share how things are going.
- Base performance reviews on previously-agreed-upon standards, position descriptions, tasks, deadlines, available resources, and intervening circumstances.
- Avoid surprises. If ongoing supervision and conflict resolution have taken place there will be no new issues raised at the review.

- Depending on the size and culture of your church, the process can be formal or informal. Do what makes sense.

- It's best to gradually include current volunteers who have not previously been reviewed. Self-assessment may work best as the system is initiated.

- Schedule reviews for a specific time or they'll be put off.

2. Benefit from the reviews.

You'll discover all kinds of benefits—to the volunteers and to your entire organization—when you start using volunteer performance reviews. Here's a short list of benefits:

- The process is a strong statement that volunteers are important and that both volunteers and organizations are held accountable to their agreements.

- Reviews are encouraging, since volunteers want to be successful and typically respond well to feedback.

- Reviews are a good time to express appreciation for volunteer efforts and acknowledge accomplishments.

- Reviews enable volunteers and volunteer ministries to renegotiate their working agreement for the next time period.

- Reviews provide an opportunity for planning to improve volunteer performance in the future (for example, training or new placement).

- Reviews allow volunteers to express concerns and escape an unfavorable situation.

- Reviews allow staff to share concerns and dismiss a volunteer if the situation requires that action.

3. Define it, with agreed-upon standards.

At the heart of a good volunteer review is a clear description of volunteer position responsibilities and success indicators. Plus, you and your volunteer should have a shared view of hoped-for outcomes and agree on what factors will contribute to those outcomes.

Performance Review Agenda

Here's an outline for a performance-review process that incorporates concept 3.

Before the Session

- Have the volunteer fill out a self-assessment form.

- Review the volunteer's position description, goals, and standards, and evaluate performance (how volunteers did their service) versus expectation (how volunteers were expected to do their service).

- Do a performance review based on the position expectation versus position performance.

During the Session

- Together, review the agreed-upon position expectations.

- Share positive feedback, and give appreciation for service.

- Volunteer: share self-assessment and assessment of church support.

- Supervisor: share assessment of volunteer's performance.

- Discuss any barriers that volunteer experienced in carrying out the position.

- Discuss future plans for the volunteer in the organization (such as position or goals).

After the Session

- Write a report for the volunteer's file.

- Follow-up on action plans or agreements made.

Barriers to Effective Performance Reviews

Betty Stallings often asks volunteer-based organizations: "What are potential barriers your organization will need to overcome to do performance reviews successfully?" Here are some of the typical responses and strategies for overcoming the barriers:

"Even our staff isn't reviewed."
Initiate reviews with staff before initiating volunteer reviews.

"We don't have any policies on reviewing volunteers."
Work together to institute policies on performance reviews and dismissal.

"Current volunteers are resisting the idea."
Involve current volunteers in developing the forms and processes.

4. Decide it, and take action.

Outcomes from volunteer performance reviews can range from applause to dismissal—by the supervisor or by the volunteer.

One way to keep volunteers continually involved in your ministry is to use reviews as a time to discuss a volunteer's readiness for a new challenge, the need for a change, or the desire to take a break for awhile. These are all legitimate reasons that a volunteer may leave your ministry, at least temporarily.

> Use reviews as a time to discuss a volunteer's readiness for a new challenge.

As a side note, when your reviews frequently point to significant problems with meeting expectations, you might look into productivity and morale. If there's been low productivity or morale on the part of the volunteer, it's important to discuss remedies. Here are some of the possible reasons you'll want to explore:

- *Is the volunteer bored with the routine?*
- *Are there personality differences between the volunteer and his or her leader or on the team?*
- *Is there idleness because of a fluctuating workload or insufficient staff?*
- *Is there a lack of interest in the work?*
- *Are the assignments poorly defined?*
- *Is there inadequate supervision and/or training?*
- *Are policies misunderstood?*
- *Is there resentment because of too much work or unrealistic deadlines?*
- *Is there poor communication within the work team (staff/volunteers)?*
- *Is the volunteer experiencing emotional stress and personal difficulties?*
- *Is participation erratic?*
- *Does the volunteer feel appreciated?*
- *Have staff or organizational changes impacted the volunteer?*
- *Is there staff resistance to utilizing volunteers?*

The flip side of evaluating a volunteer's performance is to first know whether you're meeting *their* legitimate, ongoing needs. Ask potential volunteers who have a history of serving why they left the last place they volunteered. It's not unusual to hear things such as:

"I never knew what they wanted me to do."

"I didn't even have a position description."

"I didn't know who I was responsible to, so I never knew who to go to with questions, ideas, or problems."

"They never provided any training to help me do what I was asked to do."

"Nobody ever told me if what I was doing was helpful or not."

"I was asked to do more and more, and I finally just burned out!"

Here's what volunteers repeatedly have said they want and need:

- To be carefully interviewed and appropriately assigned to a meaningful task

- To receive training and supervision to enable them to do that task well

- To be involved in planning and evaluating the program in which they participate

- To receive recognition in a way that is meaningful to them

- To be regarded as unique persons

- To be accepted as a valued member of the team

Are you currently providing those things to your volunteers? Don't assume you are—*ask*. See what volunteers tell you.

To a great extent, how a volunteer performs reflects directly on the volunteer's leader. It's the leader who provides training, equipping, encouragement, and supervision.

If you provide what volunteers legitimately need, you'll hang on to your people longer, they'll be more fulfilled and effective, and you'll see better performance. All of which translates to far happier volunteers—and fewer "problem volunteers."

Getting Started With Performance Reviews

Like most things, you get better at doing reviews the more you do them. If you're new at this, perhaps this short list of suggestions will help.

- **Do be clear about a volunteer's interests and needs.**

   When you meet with a volunteer to do an evaluation, it's not about you. It's about the volunteer. So before you present a list of things you think the volunteer could do better, show a genuine concern for the volunteer's needs.

Keep in mind that back when you or a colleague first interviewed the volunteer, you gathered information about the volunteer's interests. The review is a wonderful time to explore if the volunteer's experience has matched initial expectations.

You can get at how reality is matching expectations by exploring…

Does the volunteer's position connect with his or her interests?

Is the volunteer still interested in the position?

Does the volunteer enjoy serving in the position?

Have relationships formed that make serving in the position fun for the volunteer?

Is the volunteer satisfied with his or her level of involvement in planning, implementing, and evaluating in the ministry area?

- **Do clarify a volunteer's current interests by asking the right questions.**

  Here are some questions you'll find helpful to ask…

  What if?

  What will it take?

  Why not?

  What would be the perfect situation?

  How do you like to be treated?

  What problem(s) are we trying to solve?

  What is your goal?

  What concerns you the most?

  When are you most irritated? most satisfied?

  What's a situation when things went well?

  What do you want? What would it mean if you got it?

- **Do be professional about the review process.**

  Do performance reviews one-on-one, and respect confidentiality. Make the process feel safe for volunteers. You can hold a review in a coffee shop, in a library, or sitting on a park bench, as long as you're both comfortable and feel confident you won't be overheard. The location of the discussion isn't what makes it "professional." Your attitude does that.

- **Do provide an opportunity for volunteers to evaluate their own performance.**

  When you ask "How do you think you did?" you learn a *lot*. And while volunteers are speaking, listen attentively so you can ask follow-up questions.

- **Do be positive and focus on achievements at least as much as the areas that need improvement.**

  Again—make evaluations positive experiences.

- **Do make the discussion a dialogue, not a monologue.**

  If you're doing all the talking, you're missing much of the benefit of the review process. Be sure you ask questions and then give volunteers the encouragement and time to answer. Expect give and take, and be prepared to answer questions as well as ask them.

- **Do bring the position description and any other written materials related to the volunteer's role.**

  You'll want to review them and may, if the situation calls for it, make changes. Keep the option open for making changes to accommodate the volunteer and strengthen the volunteer ministry.

- **Do summarize what was discussed and decided.**

   It's helpful for you to get together briefly later so both you and the volunteer can review the summary. As you read through it and make sure it's accurate, you have yet another chance to clarify the information.

- **Do be open to change.**

   Things change. People change. Goals change. Use the performance review to check out whether the volunteer wants to change directions or the terms of his or her service. Maybe with a new baby in the house, it's time to take off six months or a year. Perhaps the fact the volunteer recently retired means she's open to taking on more responsibility. Not all change is bad!

And here's something you *don't* want to do…

- **Don't neglect your mentoring responsibility.**

   Mentoring and coaching can be the most rewarding parts of your role. Catch your volunteers doing good things, and applaud them. If you see something positive, reinforce the behavior and celebrate it together.

   The flip side of this is to watch for the other kinds of routine activities they may be doing—things that are just making everything harder for them.

   A brand new carpenter's apprentice once tried to nail two 2-by-4 boards together at the ends, to form a right angle. He put the boards on the ground and began nailing. But as he hit the nail, both boards would move a foot or two away from him. He kept at it for an agonizing several minutes. Eventually the foreman came over and, with an irritated look, said, "Watch." The experienced carpenter stepped on the ends of both pieces and quickly pounded in the nails.

> If you see something positive, reinforce the behavior.

Are there times like that with your volunteers? You'd better believe it. Keep your eyes wide open, and you'll see people doing all sorts of unproductive things because they're inexperienced.

They need someone to gently suggest a better approach. That's the way good coaches and mentors do it. And when important learning takes place, a warm feeling of "mission accomplished" begins to spread throughout the ministry.

Being Reactive

We do have to face the possibility: Suppose a volunteer goofs up consistently and over the long haul? Can we ever "fire" them? We hear this question in every volunteer leadership training session we present.

Our basic response is that if you're serious about holding volunteers accountable and they fail to do the job or they have inappropriate attitudes, boss others around, or procrastinate repeatedly, then you must react accordingly. Ask yourself, "What would I do if I were paying this person to do this job?"…and then do it!

First, review the position description with the individual to see if he or she is clear about what originally was agreed upon. It's amazing how often this first step clears up the problem.

Second, clarify the problem, and be explicit about your expectations.

Third, examine the alternatives together. What would it take to fix the problem? Is it a change of behavior or attitude, meeting deadlines, changing ministry roles, fixing the system, or providing training? What are the options?

Finally, agree on an alternative, and set a time line to implement it. Monitor the progress, giving support and affirmation along the way.

> What would it take to fix the problem?

If the volunteer either doesn't follow through—even after two to three chances—or is nasty about being held accountable, you may have to "fire" the person.

If you keep rescuing the individual, you both lose. This is a hard truth, but tough love may be your only option.

Here are seven guiding principles to keep in mind if you decide to let someone go...

- **Use direct dialogue.**

  You have a tough task when termination becomes necessary. It won't get any easier if you avoid the hard truths or try to candy-coat the problems this person is creating. Meet the issues head on, and avoid talking with third parties—even if the volunteer has already done this.

- **Document the process.**

  There's a great deal of emotion in play; use a process and documentation (a sample termination form is provided on page 82) to help you stay on track. You need to be able to clearly state the events and actions that brought you to the place of asking someone to leave the volunteer ministry.

- **Handle the situation privately.**

  Jesus put it like this in Matthew 18:15: "If your brother sins against you, go and show him his fault, just between the two of you. If he listens to you, you have won your brother over."

- **Search together for a better fit.**

  Maybe this particular person just needs to be redirected to find the right place. For example, if this person is having trouble getting along with others, there may be a volunteer position he or she can handle without lots of daily interpersonal interactions. Can this person do a great job of creating a website, organizing e-mails, writing the bulletin each week, or overseeing computer maintenance? Be creative in this exploration together! The so-called "problem volunteer" may become an ideal kingdom worker once his or her true abilities, skills, and passions are uncovered and put to use in the church.

- **Keep your focus on the program goals.**

> "Conflict shouldn't be a permanent barrier to Christian unity."

The conflict-solving process, even if it involves termination, isn't the end of the story. Getting the volunteer ministry back on track and the terminated volunteer placed elsewhere in God-glorifying, kingdom-building, fulfilling service are what you want. Conflict shouldn't be a permanent barrier to Christian unity.

- **Agree on a follow-up schedule.**

  You're not trying to remove this person from the church! But when volunteers feel hurt or believe an injustice has been done, they'll sometimes cut themselves off from fellowship. Be available for spiritual counsel and mentoring, and communicate clearly that the transaction wasn't personal but, instead, a systemic and organizational necessity.

- **Notify others who will be affected.**

  You'll need to tell certain members, staff, and others that the volunteer will no longer be with the ministry. Do this in an objective manner, and make sure your notification method leaves no subtle insinuations or innuendoes. Be sure you communicate *exactly* what you want to say. In most cases, you won't have to explain reasons or causes.

Finally, at the risk of overstating our case, we want to emphasize how rare it will be that anyone will ever be asked to leave your ministry. In fact, if you're putting into practice the principles outlined in this book, *you will never have to face that unpleasant task.* You see, we firmly believe that volunteer motivation and retention are the result of doing other things right—most of which you're probably already doing in an excellent way.

Among these practices are…

- Valuing relationships and celebrating them.
- Valuing experiential, applicable, and learner-centered training for volunteers.
- Respecting volunteers as full partners in ministry.
- Monitoring volunteers for signs of burnout.
- Conducting regular performance reviews.
- Fostering an environment where there's no put-down humor or victims.
- Creating a culture that volunteers can count on to be fair, forgiving, and fun.

Read that last word again…*fun!*

We use the word generously when we talk about working with volunteers because it's really the framework for effective ministry teams. Enjoy working with your volunteers. Just keep loving them and treasuring their fellowship.

1. The information in the "Key Concepts" section draws heavily upon Betty Stalling's workshop on "Evaluation." www.bettystallings.com

Sample Termination Interview

Volunteer name: _____

Date of interview: _____

Summary of reasons for termination:
(Document the events, problems, and tasks.)

_____

_____

_____

Interview Checklist:

Be sure you cover each of these items:

___ Discuss and complete this evaluation.

___ Explore alternative roles for redirection.
(If new positions were proposed, list what they were and whether they were accepted or rejected.)

___ Agree on specific follow-up plans.

___ Schedule follow-up meeting.
Date of meeting: _____ Location: _____

___ Extend continued church fellowship.

___ Pray together.
(Mutually recognize God's leading and grace in this matter.)

___ Other:_____

To Be Used at Follow-up Meeting:

___ Determine if the individual is active in ministry.
If so, where? Is the new ministry role satisfactory to the volunteer? Why or why not?

___ Determine if the individual is involved in the fellowship of the church.
Why or why not?

Encouragement Through Recognition

You're already encouraging volunteers through interviews, careful placement, and positive evaluations. Now add recognition to the mix, and delight your volunteers even more!

We tend to think of recognition as the last thing we do for a volunteer after they've finished a project and just before he or she heads off into the sunset.

Not true! In this chapter, Betty Stallings describes how recognition—and the encouragement it provides—can be infused throughout your ministries... and throughout a volunteer's experience.[1]

Betty herself caught the "disease of volunteering," as she puts it, from her father. Here is her story—and her valuable insights about recognition in volunteer ministry.

A Treasure

At the time, Betty's father was 86 years old and had lived in a skilled-care facility for nearly five years. The one thing that made him feel important was serving on different committees.

About a year earlier, he'd gone to visit Betty in California, intending to stay for a week. He got off the plane in his wheelchair, a little bag tucked onto his lap. When Betty and her father reached her house, he went right to his room to unpack, then called Betty in to see what he'd carried so carefully in the little bag on his lap.

He pulled out an undershirt and carefully unfolded it. Nestled inside was a coffee cup bearing this inscription: "You are a treasure."

"Daddy, who else knows this about you?" Betty asked.

> Daddy, who else knows this about you?

He sat up straight and said, "I'm the treasurer of the Recycling Club at the home."

Betty's first thought was that letting her dad be the treasurer of *anything* was a frightening thought.

"But then I stopped to feel gratitude," Betty says. "Some caring person had taken time to see my 86-year-old father and notice that he was, indeed, a treasure. And my father cherished the gesture enough to carry a coffee cup from Boston to California to show his daughter."

That kind of encouragement and recognition is what keeps us alive. We make an incredible impact when we remind each other what treasures we are in each others' lives, even with something as simple as a coffee cup. Those little reminders keep us going through the tough times because we know we're not alone. Somebody noticed.

Recognizing and encouraging volunteers is a huge part of your calling as the leader of a volunteer ministry. So let's dive into how you can be effective.

We'll start by thinking about a time you were—or weren't—recognized in a volunteer role.

Then we'll explore what Betty calls the "Four P's of Recognition"—making it Personal, Plentiful, Powerful, and Practical.

Next, we'll find that not all people like to be recognized in the same way, and you'll discover techniques for delivering the perfect touch at just the right time to keep your volunteers encouraged and recognized.

Finally, we'll wrap up with a list of recognition ideas you can use right away in your own volunteer ministry.

How Have You Been Recognized?

Think about your own recognition experiences...

Describe a volunteer role you've held at some time in your life. Why did you hold that position?

_____

_____

What motivated you to do—and keep doing—this position?

_____

_____

In what ways did that organization recognize you? What was meaningful, and what wasn't meaningful?

_____

_____

What did this experience teach you about recognition of volunteers?

_____

_____

What is your current philosophy about recognition? What shaped it?

_____

_____

For your recognition efforts to be encouraging to your volunteers rather than a nuisance, I'd suggest your efforts include four characteristics.

1. Recognition must be PERSONAL.

One person who filled in a chart like the one shown here concluded: "Recognition is a very personal thing. You have to know the persons you're recognizing. If you don't know them, it can be a really horrible experience. But if you know them and recognize them, it'll be an experience that will be with them forever."

Personalizing recognition efforts means you'll never again find yourself sitting through a discussion like this one:

"So, how are we going to recognize volunteers this year?"

"Let's give them plaques. I think plaques are great! People love plaques."

"Plaques? I hate plaques! Why don't we give them a flower pot to put on their desks?"

"That's hokey! Who wants flowers? They just die, and you have to throw them away."

Notice that every comment about what might be a great recognition reflects a personal bias about what the speaker enjoys or doesn't enjoy. It's not about the volunteers at all.

The best recognition offers personal validation. You place a person in the right role. Then you notice what this particular individual wants and needs, and you fulfill those wants and needs. That's 95 percent of recognition.

> If we know the person...we can zero in on a recognition that will be meaningful.

If we've put people in the wrong jobs, then our creative recognition ideas won't help much. And if we don't understand what's motivating a volunteer, we can't recognize the volunteer appropriately.

But if we know the person and what motivates him or her, we can zero in on a recognition that will be meaningful. Following are some suggestions about how to narrow down your thinking until you've got the perfect idea.

- **Make it special for just little ol' her.** If Sally begins her volunteer service on June 1st, that date is special to her. What if she received a handwritten celebration note each year on her anniversary? You've honored her and made her feel uniquely special.

- **Make it a visual feast of the feat.** Betty shares the story of how she once helped out behind the scenes with a local theater organization. She was in the background the whole time, while the actors did their thing in the spotlight. In recognition of her service, however, the cast put a picture of the production on a plaque and wrote on it: "Betty, thank you for helping make this play possible!" That plaque reminds her about the feats accomplished as a team.

- **Make it fit the personality profile.** The real challenge is to make everyone in the group feel special. But people are so different in what communicates encouragement and appreciation. How do you make sure you connect with everyone?

  Although it's possible to put together an event that contains enough diverse elements to speak to each volunteer, it only works if ahead of time you ask, "How can everyone feel special when they leave this event?"

- **Make it timely—ASAP**. The timeliness of recognition is important. The closer to the accomplishment or project, the better. That's why it's not necessarily the best way to wait until the end of the year or the close of the event to recognize people.

- **And here's a bonus idea:** To recognize someone who showed up just once—invite the person back! If it was a good one-day experience, chances are the volunteer might come back again, and you've gained a new, highly motivated volunteer.

The bottom line: Recognition doesn't take that much time, but it *does* take planning, sincerity, and action on a very personal level.

2. Recognition must be PLENTIFUL.

Like the old story about voting in Chicago: Do recognition early, and do it often. For recognition to be encouraging, it needs to be an ongoing aspect of our overall leadership style.

Encouraging recognition has to permeate your volunteer ministry and, hopefully, your church. Everyone on staff needs to be convinced of its importance, not just you. You can't be the only person recognizing others, the designated cheerleader. That won't feel right.

This means that spontaneity is just fine. Recognition will often be informal and spontaneous. And it will be more powerful for that spontaneity.

When to Recognize Volunteers

Effective recognition doesn't only happen when a project is completed. It needs to be plentiful and ongoing. Here are some quick ideas about when you can recognize people:

- At the sign-up table
- On the first day
- Daily
- Monthly
- Annually
- At the end of a project
- On special days
- On sick days
- Upon departure
- Your ideas? Jot them below:

_____

_____

_____

_____

---

3. Recognition must be POWERFUL.

Betty serves on a board that at every meeting recognizes one of its members for something they've done since the previous meeting. Sometimes it's funny, it's always spontaneous, and it's definitely effective.

Says Betty, "We all show up in case we're going to get this recognition. We know we need to be there, and because it's done at the beginning of the meeting, we know we need to arrive on time. A room full of very busy people who manage to make every meeting and on time—that's the power of even *potential* recognition!"

How Do You Say "Thanks"?

Just saying "Thank you" is powerful in itself. Here's a guide to help you clarify what you think and feel about saying thanks.

To me, saying "Thank you" means the most when...

_____

_____

Saying "Thank you" means little if...

_____

_____

The most creative way anyone has ever thanked me was to...

_____

_____

The way we usually say "Thanks" around here is...

_____

_____

Some of the people I/we need to say "Thank You" to this week are...

_____

_____

Some creative ways to do this might be...*(just brainstorm a little)*

_____

_____

What did you learn about yourself here? Discuss your ideas with other leaders. What suggestions do they have?

_____

_____

Betty attended an event years ago in which she helped the organizer. After the event, the organizer was thanking Betty for helping. As they spoke, the organizer absent-mindedly put her hand into her jacket pocket. She didn't realize there was anything in it, and Betty could tell that she was somewhat surprised to find a partial roll of Lifesavers. She smiled and handed the roll to Betty, saying, "You've been a real Lifesaver today!"

It was so small, but it was so very powerful.

4. Recognition must be PRACTICAL.

You may hear objections to the practice of recognizing volunteers, which can keep you from having a truly encouraging ministry. Here's Betty's advice for addressing those excuses—most of which fall into the "it's not practical for us" category.

- **"There's no money in the budget for this sort of thing."** Recognition doesn't have to cost a lot of money. Explain that you don't need a catered banquet—just some rolls of Lifesavers!

- **"Volunteers say they don't want or need recognition."** Except—they do. Maybe they're saying they don't need another plaque, but be assured, they'll welcome appropriate recognition.

- **"The paid staff aren't even recognized!"** In a church where paid staff are not recognized, there may not be enthusiasm for recognizing volunteers. Give it a try anyway. Even better: Recognize the paid staff, too! One church leader has shared that in her organization, the volunteers nominate staff people for recognition—which is both powerful and effective.

- **"One of our sacred cows is standing in the way of personal recognition."** Nobody *says* this, of course, but it's the problem. And you can't shoot a sacred cow unless you're prepared for lots of beef(s).

> "You can't shoot a sacred cow unless you're prepared for lots of beef(s)."

Maybe someone thinks it's undignified. Or that it diminishes the value of service if someone says "thanks." Or maybe it's as simple as the fact the church has never before recognized volunteers, and therefore, it isn't something that needs to be done now. With tact and wisdom, see if you can at least herd the sacred cow to one side of the aisle so you can slip past it.

When recognition is personal, plentiful, powerful, and practical, it encourages and edifies your volunteers. That's probably no surprise. What might be surprising, though, is how many people give of themselves as volunteers when they receive little or no encouragement or recognition at all.

Recognizing Teams As Well As Individuals

It's great to recognize individual volunteers. But don't forget that most of our volunteer efforts are, at heart, team efforts. So it's smart to find ways to regularly celebrate, affirm, and recognize the volunteer ministry team as a whole.

A common approach is to plan an annual celebration at the end of each church year. You could make it like an awards banquet for a sports team, or you could make it part of a larger service of worship and praise to God.

In any case, when it comes time to recognize and affirm team members, be sure you've developed categories of excellence. Provide recognition for various achievements and outstanding work (make these honors real and deserved). If it's a celebration strictly for the leadership team, then invite all team members, and celebrate the completion of one or more particular projects. Highlight every aspect of the success, and recognize the contributions of each person involved.

If your leadership group is small and you want to be less formal, then simply plan a dinner (or breakfast) out together. Make plans to highlight and celebrate team successes. You might also hand out mementos or small gifts, such as logo coffee mugs or gift certificates to appropriate stores.

Here are a few other ideas for encouraging and recognizing a team...

- **Start a team project scrapbook**. Include memorabilia and photographs from special projects, events, and achievements.

- **Create a recognition sheet.** Make it available for people to complete at any time. Leave space for the team member's name, the date, and a brief explanation of how that team member had a special impact on the ministry's success. Ask the person completing the sheet to sign it, and send it to the team leader. The team leader can then trumpet the accomplishments publicly.

- **Create an affirmation board.** It's the same concept as above, but post the sheets of paper where everyone can see them. Ground rule: All comments must be positive and affirming!

- **Hand out a team rose.** Start each leadership meeting with a time when members can recognize and affirm one another. Then together decide who will receive the single rose-in-a-vase for that week.

- **Schedule a team meeting as a surprise celebration.** You've heard of a surprise birthday party? How about a surprise affirmation party? Fill the meeting room with balloons, and make refreshments available. Then celebrate all the good that's been accomplished in the past month, quarter, or year. Be specific about what has happened and who did what. Consider blending in a time of praise and worship to the Lord, who guided and strengthened everyone involved.

- **Hold a staff appreciation luncheon.** Use the time to say thanks and to recognize the volunteers' efforts. Don't conduct business.

Connecting Recognition to Motivational Preference

Learn to recognize several kinds of people when it comes to motivational preference: Affiliators, Power People, and Achievers. The chart on page 93 suggests ways you could provide encouragement and recognition that was tailor-made for each of these motivational preferences.

> Encouragement is rare—and therefore precious.

Encouragement is like a breath of fresh air in the lives of volunteers. Most people simply don't hear much encouragement or receive much recognition in daily life. It's rare—and therefore precious.

Recognition Based on Motivational Type

Affiliators

Awards and Acknowledgements

- Name and photo appearing in newsletter
- Recognition in presence of family, peers
- Personal notes and verbal greetings from supervisor
- Cards for special anniversary or birthday
- Gifts and notes from clients
- Banquets, potlucks, picnics
- Attending a social event with other people

Benefits That Encourage Ongoing Commitment

- Opportunities for socialization and meeting new friends
- Personalized on-the-job training

Power People

Awards and Acknowledgements

- Public recognition (in front of peers, in media)
- Awards named for them
- Letters of commendation noting their influential achievements or impact
- Notes from influential people, community leaders, and other notables commenting on their effect on humankind

Benefits That Encourage Ongoing Commitment

- Assignments providing opportunities for influence, teaching, and interaction with high officials
- Assignments with impressive titles
- Work with a good deal of authority involved
- Board of Directors position

(continued on next page)

Achievers

Awards and Acknowledgements

- Plaques, badges, pins (tangible awards)
- Letters of special commendation on their achievement(s) to boss, newspaper, or school
- An award named in their honor
- Nomination for local, state, national awards
- Résumé documentation
- Promotion to a more responsible position

Benefits That Encourage Ongoing Commitment

- Entire responsibility delegated to them and latitude given to them on the way it is done
- Opportunities to set goals, create innovative ideas
- Work to succeed or exceed a specific goal

Encouragement and recognition will help you hang onto the volunteers who are already involved and will also create the sort of culture that attracts new volunteers. You've already built a wonderful culture as you have instituted ministry descriptions, interviews, placement, and evaluation. Excellent, encouraging recognition practices are the icing on the cake.

In the church, all the members are part of the body of Christ. We're all working toward the same mission. We all play a crucial role.

There are plenty of believers out there, willing and able to help do anything that needs doing in the church. We just need to love and care for them as Christ cares for us.

Winning Encouragement and Recognition Ideas for Volunteers

We suggest you develop recognition methods in three categories: ideas to use regularly to provide ongoing support, ideas you will use informally, and those you will use formally for special occasions.

Some of the ideas presented below are offered to "prime the pump" of your own creativity. Add your own ideas, and then plan to implement as many as possible in the future.

1. Offer ongoing support.

- Set up a suggestion box for suggestions from volunteers only.

- Implement a "release time" each week or month. This would be a chance for volunteers to pursue volunteer enrichment activities or just have some time off for rest and relaxation.

- Throughout the year, pay attention to the environment in which your volunteers labor and have meetings. Make surroundings pleasant, comfortable, and stocked with all the practical items and tools they need. (If possible, include some "luxuries.") What a morale booster this is!

- Set up support groups for your volunteers. When these groups meet, they can share their experiences, concerns, solutions, and ideas. They can pray for one another and develop their own creative ideas for mutual self-support.

- Encourage volunteers to create new ministries that will match their skills and desires to serve (rather than always slotting people into current ministries).

- Be sure your church pays the costs and expenses of any training conferences or workshops you recommend. Schedule such events regularly for increasing volunteer competency and self-confidence.

> Encourage volunteers to create new ministries.

2. Informally recognize volunteers.

- Send a birthday, anniversary, or Christmas card.

- Offer impromptu verbal affirmation; what's important is who gives it and what accomplishments are mentioned.

- Involve volunteers in the long-range planning of your church.

- Invite volunteers to church staff, planning, and other significant meetings.

- Regularly send out press releases to local media outlets. Tell all about the marvelous work of your volunteers in the various programs. Name names, and be specific about what is being accomplished. (As appropriate, also include information about how particular volunteers serve in other groups in the community. We're in this together!)

- Constantly send out thank-you notes about a job well done, no matter how small the job may have been. It deserves praise, for it was done for the kingdom.

- Praise your volunteers to their family and friends. (How could this hurt?)

- In the church bulletin, regularly or occasionally list the persons who volunteer in your church and/or the community. Regularly do this on bulletin boards and within the church newsletter, as well.

- Give small gifts occasionally, but tie them to an affirmation. Use the following examples to come up with your own individualized ideas.

> "Constantly send out thank-you notes about a job well done."

What a bright idea!
(Note stuck to a light bulb.)

No one holds a candle to you!
(Scented candle or pack of birthday candles.)

You are a LIFESAVER!
(Candy with a note.)

Thanks for raisin' the tough questions!
(Mini boxes of raisins.)

3. Formally recognize volunteers.

- Have a birthday lunch once a month to celebrate all volunteer and paid staff birthdays that occurred during that month.

- Give the volunteer a promotion to a higher-level volunteer position, a more responsible job. Make it public.

- Nominate a volunteer for community recognition.

- Give a gift of appreciation. For example: a certificate of recognition, a book, or other memento appropriate to the volunteer ministry. Other ideas for gifts include: pens, paperweights, coffee mugs, photographs, videos, gift baskets, concert/sports tickets (get them donated), a laminated copy of an article about them in the newspaper. Or consider giving coupons good for one day off without an excuse or lunch with the director.

- Provide opportunities for your volunteers to speak! Perhaps have a regular column in your church newsletter for the "Volunteer Viewpoint."

- Consider having a Volunteer of the Week (or month or year). Give special privileges or "perks" to this person—such as providing a special parking slot right next to the church entrance! Place their pictures in a prominent place.

Encouragement Based on Volunteer Roles

Keep in mind the volunteer's role when you're giving encouragement. There is a tremendous difference in volunteer roles, and few differences are as significant as this one: Does the volunteer supervise others or not?

Every volunteer position is important. Every position has its challenges. But as a ministry leader, you know what stresses can come with supervising others. And that means if you're going to support and encourage your volunteers who supervise others, you've got to *supersize* that support and encouragement!

When you're considering how to encourage a volunteer, keep in mind the environment in which the volunteer serves. Some positions have more responsibility (and perhaps more stress) associated with them than other positions might have.

Here are the three general levels of responsibility we identified earlier, and some ideas for encouraging people in each.

- **High Responsibility Volunteer Roles**

  These people are often responsible for assigning tasks to others, and actually shape areas of ministry. They have the stress of *doing* reviews as well as receiving them, so you have much in common. Make these volunteers one of your top priorities.

  Ways to encourage people in this sort of position include…

  Personally invest in these volunteers. If you have an organizational chart, it's likely these volunteers report directly to you. So it makes sense for you to be providing extra mentoring opportunities and chances for them to grow in their abilities. See if these volunteers wish to be discipled by you or another church leader; then make that happen.

  Deliberately include them in information loops. Few things are as demotivating as working in an information vacuum. You want your ministry to be a place where the right hand *does* know what the left hand is doing. The first time your volunteer assigns people to do a task that turns out to be irrelevant, motivation sinks through the floor.

  Provide stress release activities. Give the volunteer a movie ticket (or two, with an offer to have someone provide babysitting so the volunteer can take a spouse out on a date) or, if your budget is thin, a bag of microwave popcorn and gift certificate for a DVD rental. You'll have to find out what each volunteer enjoys (a pass to the zoo? pre-paid game of bowling? magazine gift subscription?) to make a personal gift, but that's the point: You took the time to find out. And you appreciate that the volunteer is making a significant contribution.

- **Medium Responsibility Volunteer Roles**

  These people are often implementing fairly defined tasks. They don't supervise other volunteers but may supervise a function—this is the volunteer who keeps the lawn mowed all summer or who keeps the kitchen organized. That function is their responsibility.

  Ways to encourage people in this sort of position include...

  Help the volunteer hone his or her skills. You honor the volunteer and the importance of what the volunteer is doing when you say, "Great job keeping the grounds looking sharp. Here's a subscription to a magazine that's all about lawn care" or a ticket to a lawn care show at the civic center.

  Join the volunteer, and ask for a demonstration. Especially if the volunteer works alone, having some company will be welcome. Plus, showing up and asking questions is affirming.

- **Low Responsibility Volunteer Jobs**

  The duties performed by these volunteers are clearly defined and specific. Often, these positions are the "bite-sized" commitments that last either for a short time or that are seemingly unimportant.

  Ways to encourage people in this sort of position include...

  Make sure they know they're important! If at all possible, have the pastor or another recognizable church leader sign letters of thanks to these volunteers. Even better: Ask the pastor to walk through the church some Sunday thanking those who are often overlooked, such as the nursery workers, greeters, and parking lot attendants.

  Give the worker a gift that connects his or her volunteer job to the larger church mission. Making the connection is critical. If the volunteer is a parking lot attendant, give him or her a keychain. If the person is a greeter, give a welcome mat for his or her home and thank him or her for making the church a welcoming place.

Improving Your Encouragement-Giving Skills

That was a good start on creative, practical recognition ideas, but more important than your doing lots of encouraging things is your becoming a consistently encouraging person. Hone your encouragement-giving skills until encouragement flows out of you naturally. Encouragement is infectious; it spreads quickly. But somebody has to get it started. Let it be you!

> "Encouragement is infectious; it spreads quickly."

If you're not convinced that an encouraging spirit (accompanied by encouraging actions) is a crucial piece of volunteer-managing character equipment, then just open your Bible. You'll find countless examples of encouragement coming not only from Jesus and other leaders but from other believers. Consider these passages:

> I long to see you so that I may impart to you some spiritual gift to make you strong—that is, that you and I may be mutually encouraged by each other's faith. (Romans 1:11-12)

> Therefore encourage each other with these words…Therefore encourage one another and build each other up, just as in fact you are doing. (1 Thessalonians 4:18; 5:11)

> Encourage one another daily, as long as it is called Today, so that none of you may be hardened by sin's deceitfulness. (Hebrews 3:13)

> Let us consider how we may spur one another on toward love and good deeds. Let us not give up meeting together, as some are in the habit of doing, but let us encourage one another—and all the more as you see the Day approaching. (Hebrews 10:24-25)

Fill your ministry with encouragement and recognition and you'll create a culture that's fair…forgiving…and fun!

Volunteers are wonderful people. They're choosing to give of themselves and their time to serve others. But that alone doesn't take away the very real, very legitimate needs they have in their own lives. With your guidance, the volunteer ministry can help meet many of your volunteers' needs even as they're serving others. And there's nothing more encouraging than having your needs met!

Volunteers are people, and as people, they have a desire to belong someplace where they are appreciated and valued. You can provide that.

They want to know their opinions matter. As you listen deeply, you'll provide that.

They want to give themselves to something bigger than themselves. As you connect them with appropriate volunteer positions in the church, you'll help them serve in the kingdom of God.

They want to be challenged, to grow, to become excellent in doing things that matter. The volunteer positions you'll help them find and the training you'll help them receive will let that happen.

The encouragement that comes from participating in the volunteer ministry is more than a passing "feel-good" experience. You're more than a cheerleader who rallies the troops. What happens in a volunteer's heart can be a life-changing experience. It can build new skills, rekindle old passions for service, and encourage lasting relationships—including a relationship with Jesus Christ and his church.

Now let's talk about how you can build a volunteer-equipping ministry that's *energized*—that's going to go the distance!

1. The content of this chapter draws heavily from Betty Stallings' Volunteer Management Program video presentation, *Recognition: Letting People Know You Noticed.* www.bettystallings.com

The People-Energized Volunteer Ministry

An energized volunteer ministry is powered by people—both the church leadership and church membership. Here's how to involve people you need in a core team that gets things done.

Some evening after everyone else has left the building, walk through the facility where your church meets. Perhaps you have your own building; maybe you rent or borrow a space. It doesn't matter—just go when the lights are dim and the rooms are quiet.

What do you see?

You see tables and chairs. Books and curriculum. Scuffed tiles and empty nursery cribs. Stuff. You see stuff. Lots of stuff.

But what you *don't* see is the church.

The "church"—the bride of Christ—is made up of people. *We're* the church, not the stuff we use to make programs happen. Nothing you see or touch or taste as you make your tour of the empty facility is designed to last for eternity (though the janitor might disagree about the dried gum shoved up under the tables). Only people are made to last forever.

And at church, without people nothing happens.

In your volunteer ministry, without people nothing happens.

People are the point, so involve them!

We'd like to suggest that you be intentional about involving several groups of people as you launch or revitalize your volunteer-equipping ministry involvement.

> People are the point, so involve them!

- The first group is church leaders. These are people who, quite simply, have influence. Others tend to follow these people whether or not the leaders have formal leadership positions. Their opinions are sought in decision-making and problem-solving.

- The second group is the church membership. These are people who have a stake in your congregation and identify with the church and its ministries. They have gifts to give and ministries to provide—but they may not know how or where. The vast majority of your volunteers will come from this group of people.

First, let's take a look at how involving church leaders can energize your volunteer ministry.

Involving Church Leaders

When church leaders get involved, the program is energized. A leadership-powered volunteer ministry happens when most, if not all, of these identified leaders are making decisions that support volunteer equipping.

What does it look like when the leaders in your church plug into your volunteers and provide power and support? It looks like this...

- There's encouragement for the ministry—both privately in conversations and publicly from the pulpit and in church-wide written communications.

- Resources flow to the ministry. Because the value of the ministry is understood and appreciated, needed resources (an office, supplies, time with the pastor) are available.

- There's personal involvement from leaders. When there's an appreciation banquet for volunteers, church leaders attend. When volunteers are asked to stand and be recognized in the church service, church leaders lead the applause. And when the ministry needs help, church leaders step up to personally respond.

Having church leaders actively involved is important because, by definition, where leaders go, others follow. Your church's leaders define the congregation's priorities not only by what they say but by what they do. Where do they devote their time and attention? What church ministries get their undivided attention? What ministries get enthusiastic mentions on Sunday morning?

> "Your church's leaders define the congregation's priorities."

If the volunteer ministry is among those favored ministries, the congregation will begin to think of it the same way.

As you develop volunteer ministry, keep in mind you need the full understanding and support of church leadership. You need it in part because the volunteer ministry is unique—it doesn't reside in just one ministry area of the church. It's not the exclusive property of the children's ministry or the administrative area. It intersects with all ministries within your church because when there's a ministry, there are usually volunteers. The person leading your volunteer ministry needs access to *all* ministry leaders within your church.

When there's a program or ministry in the church that isn't powered by leadership, there's often a poor outcome. Consider the following true story.

A Story Without a Happy Ending

This story begins with a group of nine committed volunteers who wanted to bring a midweek children's program to their church. The program already existed in other churches, so the volunteers took vacation time from their jobs to go and receive training in how to organize and run the program.

The volunteer team met almost weekly for months to get the program up and running, and one of the pastors was committed enough to travel with them to receive training.

It looked like all systems were go, and everything was running along like clockwork. The team recruited more than 35 volunteers to be part of the midweek ministry, from working in the kitchen to providing meals for the children and volunteers, to teaching a Bible study curriculum.

The first few months of the ministry went well. Both the leaders and children were having fun. Attendance stayed high and enthusiastic... until something changed.

The church leaders who had been so involved and excited about the program quit participating. The church staff had other programs to run, and before long, the midweek program fell off of their radar screen. Even the pastor who'd been trained to help run the program faded away.

Soon the volunteers noticed that paid staff wasn't participating, and the volunteers started to feel ignored. When the program's second semester was launched, enrollment of children dipped, and it became increasingly difficult to recruit and retain adult volunteers. Church leaders were actively soliciting volunteers for *other* programs, since the midweek effort was established.

Within the year, a very painful decision was made to abandon the midweek program. The dedication of many volunteers was essentially negated, and to this day, some of those volunteers have not become fully involved in other work of the church.

Was the decision to cancel the program a good one? a bad one? We don't know—but we *do* know one reason the program faltered was that key leaders pulled out, resulting in volunteers losing focus and energy.

The senior pastor can't be personally involved in every church program. That's not practical. But for church ministries to be connected and powered by leadership, *some* leader needs to be in the loop.

We also know of ministries where senior leadership participated for a time and then left—*but that was part of the plan*. Everyone knew that the pastor wouldn't stay on the worship committee long-term; the pastor's role was understood to be temporary, so when he left, it was with the blessings of everyone involved. He'd made his contribution during the vision and mission stages of the committee formation; now he was done. No one felt abandoned.

Had the team putting together the midweek program asked some hard questions (listed below), expectations would have been realistic and the level of commitment from leadership understood from the beginning. And the program may well have survived the leadership crisis it experienced.

Without the support of church leaders, volunteers feel unsupported and unrecognized for their efforts and contribution. When leaders aren't actively demonstrating support, the congregation tends to have a lukewarm commitment to a church ministry. For better or worse, church members take their cues from church leaders.

> **For better or worse, church members take their cues from church leaders.**

So you want the volunteer ministry to be energized by people in leadership. You *need* to have the volunteer ministry energized by people in leadership. How do you make that happen?

How to Create a Leadership-Energized Volunteer Ministry

There are two steps in gaining leadership energy for your program: Engage church leaders from the beginning, and keep leaders in the information loop at all times.

- **Engage leaders from the beginning.**

  Meet with church staff to determine their level of interest and commitment to a volunteer ministry. In the meeting, discuss the leaders' vision for the volunteer program and how they see the program impacting the church's mission. Share information freely, and allow time for dialogue. This meeting is a great time to determine who on the staff will serve as an "invested individual" and participate in the vision statement and meetings (more about those later in the next two chapters).

  You can expect to hear that a volunteer ministry is important. Those words will be comforting, but what also counts is how church leaders will become involved and stay involved as the ministry develops.

It's fair to ask some hard, probing questions:

- *How do you think God intends for our church members to be engaged in service to one another and the community?*

- *How do you think our congregation will benefit from a more organized volunteer ministry? (Describe what a "more organized volunteer ministry" would look like.)*

- *What specific things can we improve when it comes to getting our members more involved in the work of the church?*

- *How would being more involved in a volunteer ministry benefit the members of our church?*

- *How much time will you commit to getting this effort started, and then to providing ongoing support?*

- *Where do you see the volunteer ministry residing in the organization? Who will be responsible for it?*

- *What resources will the church devote to the ministry (for example, financial support, people, space, equipment)?*

> "Don't be hesitant to directly ask for support."

As you discuss the leaders' commitment to the volunteer ministry, don't be hesitant to directly ask for support. Be prepared to define "support" so leaders know precisely what you're asking. Here are some possible questions that get at specific ways to provide support.

- *Will you frequently refer to the volunteer ministry in meetings and from the pulpit?*

- *Will you describe the impact of the volunteer ministry on how our church is accomplishing the church's mission?*

- *Will you tell people you expect them to be involved in service through the volunteer ministry?*

- *Will you attend some or all of the meetings for the volunteer ministry? If not, what church leader will?*

- *Will you periodically write articles for the church newsletter about the volunteer ministry and what it's accomplishing?*

These sort of actions set an example for the rest of the congregation and also cement your relationship with church leadership. They energize the ministry!

- **Keep leadership in the information loop.**

  When we're thinking and praying about something, it naturally takes a place of priority in our lives. We identify with it.

  That's one reason you want to keep church leaders in the information loop—so they'll have the volunteer ministry top of mind. They'll remember to pray for you and the ministry. They'll be inclined to send possible volunteers to you. They'll think of the ministry as a solution to challenges that arise in church programming.

  But delivering information—reports, briefings, and statistics—isn't the only way to keep in touch with your church leaders. Consider these practical approaches for closing the distance between your leadership and the volunteer ministry:

  - Create a recognizable logo for the volunteer ministry, and use it often. It will remind leaders that you're out there and available.
  - Send simple, quick-read e-mails with messages about the volunteer ministry. Make the messages encouraging and upbeat.
  - Create a button for people involved in the ministry to wear on their lapels.
  - Insert a page of accomplishments or outcomes from the volunteer ministry in the church newsletter.
  - Send birthday cards celebrating the milestones in the volunteer ministry to the leaders to share successes of the ministry (for example: "Happy birthday to our volunteer ministry! We're officially one year old!").
  - In the church newsletter, highlight leaders, and talk about their connection to the volunteer ministry.
  - Include a celebration during National Volunteer Week. (In the United States, it's usually in April.)
  - Give a volunteer ministry statistic during each leadership meeting.
  - Include key leaders on the initial core team.

> **Be intentional about bringing the volunteer ministry to the attention of your church leaders.**

Be intentional about bringing the volunteer ministry to the attention of your church leaders. You aren't bragging when you tell of the success volunteers are having in doing effective ministry. You aren't lacking humility if you draw attention to what God is doing in the volunteer ministry. Rather, you're celebrating a ministry that will bless both your volunteers and the church leaders who rely on those volunteers.

Consider this passage, where the Bible writer shares his joy at hearing how a friend is being faithful in his ministry and message:

> *It gave me great joy to have some brothers come and tell about your faithfulness to the truth and how you continue to walk in the truth. I have no greater joy than to hear that my children are walking in the truth.* (3 John 3:3-4)

Your pastor feels the same way. Brighten your pastor's day with a good report about what's happening in the volunteer ministry.

Involving Church Members

When church members get involved, the program is energized. We like to think of creating a membership-energized volunteer ministry as creating a groundswell.

A groundswell is actually a wave in the ocean—a powerful wave in the open sea, the result of an earthquake, a storm, or another event far away. The wave can travel thousands of miles, and while they're sometimes hard to notice on the open sea, they hit the shore with surprising force.

Perhaps that's why the term "groundswell" has come to mean unexpected support that builds for a cause or political candidate. At first you may not even notice the momentum building, but then it's there, and it's powerful.

You want your volunteer ministry to have a "groundswell" feel to it. That is, it needs to have an exciting, excellent reputation that draws people to it.

It needs to build power as it travels along. You want the energy to grow as it radiates throughout the congregation and for people to be *clamoring* to join as volunteers.

A groundswell of support is spread over a large number of people. It doesn't depend on one person climbing up on a soapbox and expounding on the virtues of the volunteer ministry.

Groundswells can't be manufactured. They come about because something happens—an event, a success, a testimonial—that generates a response in people.

You can't *make* it happen...but you can *encourage* it. And a great place to begin encouraging support is by creating a volunteer ministry core team that will in time energetically help spread the word about the ministry.

In the same way that the senior pastor can't participate in every church ministry and planning meeting, neither can every church leader get involved on your core team. In fact, you don't *want* every church leader serving on the core team. The group would be too large and unwieldy. Nothing would ever be decided.

You're looking for a small group of people who'll infuse the ministry with the people-power that flows from the members of your congregation. You're looking for people who will be the hands and hearts of the volunteer ministry. You're looking for people who'll help you enjoy the benefits of synergy.

> You're looking for people who will be the hands and hearts of the volunteer ministry.

Synergy: 1 + 1 = 3

We often use the word "synergy" to describe what happens when people work together and a groundswell forms. Synergy is an equation that lets you add one plus one and get a total of three. Odd math, but it represents what happens when people join forces to work together on a core team or other project. Properly focused, their output is greater than the sum of the individuals working independently.

It's not a new concept. God describes synergy this way: "For where two or three come together in my name, there am I with them" (Matthew 18:20). One plus one equals three.

> " Want to get people involved? Start by forming a core team. "

God calls us to pray and do his work, and he powers our efforts. That's the same power that, in turn, can support and sustain your volunteer program. It's what lets your volunteer program thrive.

Want to get people involved? Start by forming a core team.

Creating a Volunteer Ministry Core Team

A core team is a small team given responsibility for a specific assignment with specific goals. And that means you've got to be *very* clear about the specific task you're asking people to accomplish. What exactly do you want people to do?

We'd like to suggest that you form a core team around actually leading your volunteer ministry, not around just the fact-finding portion of the process. In many churches—especially churches of 500 members or fewer—it's most effective when the core team actually takes on key responsibilities such as creating position descriptions for volunteer roles and doing interviewing.

As far as recruiting core team members, you've talked with church leaders who may serve on your core team. You know people who are already volunteers serving in the church. These people are possible core team members. But you'll have to ask them.

You're asking for a commitment to work with you as you establish a volunteer ministry or as you take your existing ministry through some significant changes. You want people to help you pray for God to work his will in and through the program. To help you design the steps necessary for achieving new outcomes for the program. To help you evaluate the progress along the way.

Your core team will get the new or revitalized volunteer ministry up and running and then, when the time is right, transition into a different role — providing support and advice to the person selected to be the director of the volunteer-equipping ministry.

Keep in mind that whoever is serving as the director does *not* want to be in the role as a "lone ranger." The director needs support and help! The core team will need to shift to a new focus, but there will always be a need for the involvement of good people who are committed to the ministry and its success. Clearly, selecting the right people for the core team is important. In the next few pages we'll give you some advice about how to make sure you're pulling together the right team.

The following chart will help you think through a list of "invested individuals" who should be part of your core team. Your life will be easier if you keep the list short, but remember, if you expect your pastor to support the vision statement later, you'd best get your pastor on the core team early on.

Invested Individuals—Analysis Chart for Creating a Core Team

Who are "invested individuals" in the volunteer ministry (could be individuals or groups)?	What is their stake in the volunteer ministry (e.g., they control the resources)?	How can we get them to support and participate in the volunteer ministry?
_____	_____	_____
_____	_____	_____
_____	_____	_____
_____	_____	_____

There's simply no better way to energize your volunteer ministry with people-power than to carefully create a core team. Here are three things to keep in mind as you think about your team.

1. Don't think you can make it without a core team.

It's tempting to just push on ahead without a core team, but you won't last long if you make that mistake.

The job of creating or changing the volunteer ministry culture, even in a small church, is just too big. Plus, when you involve people in the creation of a ministry, they're more likely to go to great lengths to see it survive and thrive.

The people on your core team will protect and promote the volunteer ministry in your church and community. They'll make sure the ministry is supported, organized, improved, and sustained. They'll provide the prayer, commitment, and effort that makes your program thrive. They'll energize your ministry!

> Remember, you're not in a sprint; you're in a marathon.

Remember, you're not in a sprint; you're in a marathon. You can't do it all alone or run the race without help.

2. Charter your core team.

Chartering is the process of becoming crystal clear as to what the core team exists to accomplish. It identifies the commitment needed and the outcomes desired—what you intend to accomplish. Any group that intends to collectively work toward a desired outcome can benefit from the process, and an effective task force requires it.

The best charters emerge from discussions, and the following questions will lead your potential core team members to a thorough understanding of what's going to be required of the core team.

- *Who is responsible for our core team's outcomes (for example, the elders, board, pastor)? How will we interact with that person?*

- *How will our core team be known in the church? What's our name?*

- *What's the mission of our core team? (Note: It will be different from the mission of the volunteer ministry.) What's our mission statement? Why do we exist?*

- *How will we know when we've succeeded and our work is complete? What's our vision for our preferred future? What outcomes do we desire to see?*

- *What authority does our core team have? What can we do on our own, and for what must we seek approval?*

- *Who on our core team will call meetings, communicate with the rest of the church, and perform other duties? What duties need to be accomplished?*

- *How long does our core team expect to exist?*

- *How will decisions be made on our core team (for example, by consensus, majority vote, or other)?*

- *How will we conduct our core team interactions? What are the ground rules for our meetings?*

- *To whom must our core team report about progress? How will we do that?*

- *How will we measure progress on our core team?*

- *How will we obtain feedback on our effort, and what will we do with that feedback?*

- *How will we celebrate our successes as a core team?*

- *With whom should we communicate and send meeting notes (absent core team members, church ministry area leaders, among others)?*

Once you've talked through your shared understanding of the answers, ask each potential member to decide if he or she wants to sign on to work toward those goals.

Be clear that you want people to make an *informed* decision about serving on the core team. If, at the end of the meeting, someone chooses not to join, bless him or her and bid farewell.

Ask the remainder of the people to finish the charter process with you.

If you're thinking this might take some time, you're right. Plan on a 2½-hour meeting. But it's time well spent, as this first core team meeting begins the work of creating the volunteer ministry or taking your existing ministry to the next level.

> "Get agreements at the *front* end of your time together."

In the long run, it saves time to discuss these issues and to get agreements at the *front* end of your time together. If you wait until later, groups of people working together may become confused and experience conflict.

We call this "going slow to go fast"—going slow in the beginning of the process to go faster during implementation. Trust us, it's better to move slowly at the start so you don't speed along only to hit a wall later.

Sum up your answers to the discussion questions noted on pages 115 and 116. They'll become your charter. As soon as practicably possible, put the summary in front of people and ask them to sign it—formalizing the process.

See page 166 for a sample Core Team Charter Covenant.

3. When the time comes, transition the core team.

Once the core team has completed its initial work, don't let the core team members wander off into the sunset. Instead, pause to celebrate! Throw a party! Make the transition a time of fun and joy as you thank people for a job well done.

Provide a time for refreshments and swapping stories, for core team members to affirm each other. And if you've already identified the person who will be directing the volunteer ministry, let that person soak up the history of the core team.

Be sure every member of the core team feels valued and appreciated. These are people who've energized your program—they deserve heartfelt thanks. They've provided leadership and accountability as your church started on the road to experiencing significant change.

And hold this thought in mind: The director of the volunteer-equipping ministry needs an advisory committee or a board. The members of your core team are people you may want to ask to serve in that capacity. They've demonstrated they're committed to the success of the ministry, they're willing to work, and they've likely formed relationships with each other.

Energize your volunteer ministry by making room for people not just as "workers," but as leaders. Let your core team pull together those people God has gifted to help shape and reshape the ministry.

There's energizing power in a ministry built to thrive—and to thrive, it must be more than just *your* ministry.

The Prayer-Energized Volunteer Ministry

An energized volunteer ministry is powered by prayer, both personal and corporate. Here's how to plug your ministry into this power source.

Have you ever run out of gas? been driving down the highway and suddenly the engine of your car started to skip and cough, and then you could hear nothing but the wind whistling past?

Running out of gas turns any cross-country drive into a hike to the closest gas station. Because no matter how powerful your car's engine, no matter how important you or your trip are, if you run out of fuel, you're going nowhere. You're stopped cold.

There's no question about how important your volunteer ministry is—it has the ability to literally revolutionize your church. If over the course of the next few years the number of people in your church who volunteer doubled, imagine the impact. *That's* significant.

And there's no question about how important this trip you're making is. It's vital. You're establishing or improving a ministry that will help people enter into ministry and service. That's *amazingly* significant.

So don't risk running out of gas.

Even being energized by people isn't enough to sustain you for the journey. You need something more.

You need prayer.

You need prayer.

Something to Pray About

When Jesus called his disciples, he ushered them into a life of service and obedience. He expected them to follow where he led. They entered into lives of ministry.

Plus, they were expected to bring others along with them. Not only did *they* have to get on board with Jesus' vision; they were told to recruit additional volunteers, too.

The body of Christ—the church—is a service organization. Ministry is in the church's very DNA. For a Christian to be involved in service is the natural state of things—it's how we were created to live.

Consider this observation from Dennis Campbell, from the book *A Guide to Prayer for All God's People:*

> *The call to ministry is a basic idea in the life of the church. The Greek word from the New Testament is* diakonia. *Its meaning is service. To be a member of the community of those who follow Jesus is to be part of a community committed to service.*

If your church is like most, it *needs* an energized, thriving volunteer ministry! The ministry helps engage church members in significant service, which means you'll help your church *be* the church. It's a high calling to prayerfully, intentionally connect people with volunteer opportunities.

So understand this: *You're in ministry.* Whether you're paid staff or unpaid staff, you're in ministry. Whether you place fifty volunteers this year or just one, *you're in ministry.*

And like any person in ministry, *you need prayer!* You've got things to pray about—both for yourself and your role in this ministry and for the volunteer ministry. To create and sustain a volunteer ministry in your church, you want God's guidance. You *need* God's guidance.

It's tempting to think of the volunteer ministry as secondary to *real* ministry. After all, you don't decide if the church will launch a new building campaign, call on the sick, or do counseling with discouraged people.

But you may well be called on to create ministry descriptions for the volunteers who do those things and to interview those people. Those front-line ministry positions may never be filled without your active involvement.

That makes your volunteer ministry not just a behind-the-scenes administrative function; it's a front-line ministry.

So let us say it again: *You need the power of prayer*. You need God's guidance. You need the discernment that comes with prayer.

But you already pray, right? What Christian doesn't?

What we're suggesting isn't that you casually pray about the volunteer ministry, but that you intentionally create a ministry that's *energized and powered* by prayer.

How to Design a Prayer-Energized Volunteer Ministry

A *prayer-energized* ministry is one where prayer comes first. It's not just something we do after we've gotten ourselves into a pickle! It *precedes* our actions and opens our hearts to hearing God tell us what ministry is needed and how we can fulfill that ministry.

Prayer helps ensure that our volunteer ministry comes out of God's agenda for our congregation and not our own agendas. Ministries based on our own agendas are dependent solely on our presence and commitment. As soon as we become discouraged, move away, or get stressed, the ministry falters. That's not the sort of ministry that will thrive.

Ground your volunteer ministry in prayer and you'll reap short- and long-term benefits. And since the work of your volunteer ministry is the work of the Lord, why not let God run it?

Here are some suggestions about how to design a prayer-energized ministry.

> Here are some suggestions about how to design a prayer-energized ministry.

1. Begin by valuing prayer.

How important is prayer to you? to members of your team? to your church? We don't mean to be insulting by asking, but those are important questions. It's not necessarily true that every church places a high value on intercessory prayer—asking for God to enter into situations to make his will known and to affect outcomes and people.

The issues that accompany launching or revitalizing a volunteer ministry can be a tremendous catalyst for prayer. A vital prayer life will be a lifeline for your faith through what's coming in the months ahead.

Recognize this: Not everyone in your church will feel the need to join you in prayer for the volunteer ministry. Probably not everyone in your church prays regularly. Some people pray infrequently at best.

We point out those obvious truths because for your ministry to be successfully energized by prayer, it *doesn't* require that every person in your church pray and fast for the ministry. That would be great—but it's not essential. What *is* essential is that you and a group of people who are drawn to the ministry agree to pray for God's guidance and direction and that you listen to God's voice.

And don't be mistaken: This isn't just a matter of tradition or habit. Prayer is an energizing force that can create enormous changes in and through your team.

Consider what we read in the book of James:

> Is any one of you in trouble? He should pray. Is anyone happy? Let him sing songs of praise. Is any one of you sick? He should call the elders of the church to pray over him and anoint him with oil in the name of the Lord. And the prayer offered in faith will make the sick person well; the Lord will raise him up. If he has sinned, he will be forgiven. Therefore confess your sins to each other and pray for each other so that you may be healed. The prayer of a righteous man is powerful and effective. (James 5:13-16)

From the very beginning, when you're creating a vision for your volunteer ministry, there's a central place for prayer. There's nothing more important than making sure your vision reflects what God wants to do with your ministry, that you're in harmony with God's vision. That involves asking God what he wants to do with and through you, and it mandates listening for an answer. As Charles Colson states in his book *The Body: Being Light in the Darkness:* "Prayer is the act by which the community of faith surrenders itself, puts aside all other concerns, and comes before God Himself."

2. Be disciplined in praying for your volunteer ministry yourself.

You're a key person God is using to launch or improve your volunteer ministry, so be available to God. Schedule daily time for prayer the same way you'd schedule time for anything else that's important to accomplish.

Countless books and resources are designed to help you improve your prayer life and deepen your understanding of prayer's power. Explore using one or more of those resources, or simply do this: Every day, come before God and say, "Here I am, your person in my world. I'm available for your use today. What do you have to teach me? How do you want to use me?"

You'll be amazed at how God answers those prayers.

> *"For I know the plans I have for you,"* declares the Lord, *"plans to prosper you and not to harm you, plans to give you hope and a future."* (Jeremiah 29:11)

3. Pray corporately.

Ask the leaders of ministry areas to pray for the volunteer ministry at each staff meeting, and contact whatever prayer chain or intercessory prayer ministry exists in your church. Not only will there be regular, disciplined prayer for the volunteer ministry but volunteers who already work with you will know someone is praying for them.

And there's another benefit: You can be certain the direction you understand from God for your volunteer ministry is *collectively* discerned. We once heard Sam Leonard, from the Alban Institute, say it well:

> *Hearing the will of God individually that is not tested in community can lead to madness...This is personalized theology—"the blood of Christ for me"—not for us. Volunteer work needs two "yeses": called by God and called by the church.*

When you understand that it's God's will that you move the volunteer ministry a particular direction, you can test your discernment with others. Share with them what you've prayed and how you heard God speaking to you. Corporate prayer helps you know you're faithfully following God's lead.

> **Identify a team of people who will become prayer partners for the volunteer ministry.**

Identify a team of people who will become prayer partners for the volunteer ministry. Seek out individuals with enthusiasm for the volunteer ministry, others with deep spiritual discipline, and still others who have some experience (successfully and unsuccessfully) in trying to organize volunteers in the church.

Create a discipline or process for the individual and corporate prayer effort. Choose specific times, places, and methods for keeping partners in prayer. Prayer partners can meet for prayer time or make a covenant to pray at a certain time of each day.

Recognize and affirm that people pray in different ways and that this is not only acceptable but valuable. Suggest that people may want to regularly ask God to help them notice with new eyes the gifts and resources of the church and the needs of the local community and world. Some may want to keep a short journal of these new insights. If a particular phrase or section of Scripture stands out as relevant to God's call to the church, encourage them to make a note of the passage and their new understanding so they can share that later with others.

Let everyone involved in praying for the volunteer ministry know that the goal of this prayer process is to develop an openness to God's leading of the ministry so it can function the way God intends.

You want to join the psalmist in declaring…

> I am your servant; give me discernment that I may understand your statutes. (Psalm 119:125)

Share the results of your individual prayer experiences with each other. This will provide the opportunity for the testing of discernment from prayer, and you'll achieve both yeses: called by God and by the church.

Keep people praying for the volunteer ministry by keeping information regarding the volunteer ministry in front of them. Send out daily or weekly messages about the program to focus prayers on pressing issues. Be creative in all the ways you can put those reminders in place: e-mail, cards or postcards, and telephone calls all can work. Create bookmarks, lapel buttons, or stickers your church members might use. We've even seen colorful and creative refrigerator magnets used to keep the volunteer ministry in front of people.

4. Pray specifically.

It's helpful to give people something specific to pray about. Following are some topics you can share to prompt collective prayer. Ask prayer partners to pray for…

- God's vision for the work of volunteers in your congregation.
- Church leaders to accurately identify the needs in your church, community, and world that could be met by volunteers in your congregation.
- Your congregation's commitment to ministry and service.
- Your staff's ability to support the volunteer ministry.
- The wisdom of individuals who are helping build and lead the volunteer ministry.
- The guidance of the Holy Spirit in the volunteer ministry.

- A fair distribution of work among your church's membership so the 80/20 rule does *not* prevail (20 percent of the volunteers doing 80 percent of the work).

- Increasing support of the volunteer ministry by the congregation.

- An ongoing renewal of volunteers.

- New connections to form with marginal members who could benefit spiritually from serving as volunteers.

   Again, I tell you that if two of you on earth agree about anything you ask for, it will be done for you by my Father in heaven. For where two or three come together in my name, there am I with them. (Matthew 18:19-20)

> "Here are some practical ways to keep your ministry energized by prayer."

5. Keep praying.

An ongoing dialogue with God about your volunteer ministry invites God to continue providing energy, wisdom, and compassion. You'll need all three!

Here are some practical ways to keep your ministry energized by prayer…

- Ask existing small groups within your church to adopt you as an ongoing prayer concern. Keep them in the loop about issues for which you'd like prayer.

- In the church newsletter or bulletin, share some meaningful outcomes of the ministry (for example, the growth a volunteer experienced in doing a new activity).

- Include the volunteer ministry as a prayer concern during worship services.

- Include prayer requests in your church newsletter. This will also serve as a way to inform the congregation of what is happening in the ministry. It may even end up serving as a recruitment tool.

- Begin all volunteer ministry meetings with prayer.

- Personally take time daily to pray about the volunteer program.

It's important you stay in prayer and that you're confident you're hearing God about your church's volunteer ministry, especially if you're just beginning a ministry. This is actually hard to do, because it's a natural human tendency to jump in and begin working on tasks as soon as a critical level of enthusiasm is reached. There may be other people in your church who are urging you to move ahead.

But prayer *precedes* action. Pray often, individually and collectively sharing the insights God has provided to direct you in service. Then act, create, and continue to pray for your volunteer ministry. Have the patience to wait for God's guidance, and submit to God's will no matter how much you think you know or how certain you are that your way is the best way.

Pray as if your volunteer ministry depended on it.

In many ways, it does.

The Goal- and Objective-Energized Volunteer Ministry

You're charged up and ready to move toward your vision. Here's how to take the next steps by creating goals and objectives.

You're energized—by people and prayer—and now it's time to put some wheels under your efforts to equip volunteers for ministry.

That happens when your core team develops goals and objectives... and it's time to do that.

You might typically use different terminology, but let's look at one definition of *goal:* This is the end you're aiming for. It's where you want to go. Goals are short-term actions by which you'll accomplish your mission. Or you might simply ask yourself, "What are we *doing* about our mission this year?" A goal is a broad statement that defines the "why" of your ministry.

The first draft of goals are almost always vague and hard to measure. For example, your church might set a goal of "sharing faith in our neighborhood and community." Good intention, but how will you know when you've reached the goal? When everyone has been handed a brochure about the church? When everyone has made a faith commitment to Christ?

When goals get specific, they become useful. A goal that has been sharpened and honed is sometimes called an objective. We think of it as simply a *good* goal—but let's use the term *objective* as you work with your task force.

> When goals get specific, they become useful.

When a goal meets all the criteria described below, it has been promoted to "objective"; your core team will have something to celebrate!

Here's how we'll define *objective*: An objective is a goal that has become a definite, measurable target. An objective includes standards of performance and achievement both for your area of ministry and for the people involved.

For example, the church with the goal of sharing their faith in their community can make their vague goal an objective by asking and answering questions such as:

- *How exactly will we share our faith?*
- *What outreach events will we hold that are geared toward our community?*
- *When will we hold these outreach events?*
- *How many such events will we hold this year?*
- *Exactly who do we want to reach—what neighborhood, what age range of individuals, what ethnic group?*

If you've ever driven through tall mountains, you know about switchbacks— roads that turn back on themselves as they zigzag up the face of a mountain. Because the roads climb the mountain gradually, cars can make the trip.

The *goal* of a driver is simply to reach the top of the peak. The switchbacks are like *objectives*—short, manageable, measurable steps to help drivers reach their goal.

When it comes to volunteers, many churches forget the switchbacks and just try to drive right up the sheer mountainside. No wonder so many volunteers burn out quickly!

How to Turn a Goal Into an Objective

We'd like to suggest five yardsticks against which you can measure goals and objectives. If a goal measures up in all five areas, it's an objective. Promote it, celebrate it, and use it. But if the goal comes up short in any of these five areas, run it through your core team again to shape it up.

And be brutal: Promote no goal before it's ready! If people are fuzzy when they're *talking* about a goal, wait until they try to *act* on it. That's when things break down in a *big* way!

1. Is the goal specific?

How many? By when? At what cost? How will you know when you're done? Those are all things you need to know before you can delegate a goal to someone.

Some people become concerned that if you're too specific about goals (or any other part of your planning), you're not trusting God to lead your ministry. I don't think that's the case. By all means, ask God if it's his will for you to add four volunteer Sunday school teachers by next July, or if it's his will that you recruit an additional 12 male voices into the choir before you start Christmas program rehearsals. If you sense that the answer is "yes," then move ahead with the goal you've prayed about.

On the other hand, if you're not clear about your goal, how can God respond clearly? If you're praying, "Lord, please help me know if you want us to make the nursery safer and more efficient," I can tell you right now the answer to that prayer is yes. God loves children. God cares about children. Of *course* he'll want you to do the best possible job in the nursery.

But if you meant, "Help me know if you want us to add Mary and Jack to our nursery staff," that's an entirely different question.

And being specific is helpful in more ways than simply guiding your prayer life. It also lets you know when you've completed what you set out to do.

If you only say, "We need more volunteers to staff the nursery," are you successful if you recruit just one? If you don't say "We need to recruit those volunteers by April 1 of next year," then do the people charged with accomplishing that task have forever to get it done? You'll quickly learn that while specific seems scary (remember, someone might hold you accountable), it's actually a key element to reaching your objectives.

2. Is the goal measurable?

If you're specific—stating how much and by when—you've got good measurements in place. A goal is measurable if it includes clear wording about budget, growth, time, and achievement—all the specifics that might impact the goal.

Don't be quick to slap those measurements onto goals, though. If you want to achieve a goal by June 1, have a good reason for selecting that date. If you want to define "success" as hitting 100 percent participation in the church work day, is it a reasonable goal? Before you formalize the numbers and dates associated with your goals, consider the next yardstick measurement, #3.

> A goal is measurable if it includes clear wording about budget, growth, time, and achievement.

3. Is the goal challenging but achievable?

Set realistic goals. You want to help people stretch but not be stretched so far they snap. Being handed an unachievable goal can be demoralizing and defeating. If the numbers are too big or the time too short, your volunteers may feel like huge failures—*even when they've done great work.*

Although you want to challenge your volunteers, you also want to be realistic when determining what you'll accomplish. For example, maybe you've been involved in a fundraiser for a new church building. Your stated goal was to raise $1,500,000 in two years. At the end of two years, you'd raised $1,350,000. Did you succeed or fail?

You didn't reach the goal, so maybe the correct answer is that you failed.

But do you want your team of fundraisers—people who managed to raise $1,350,000 in two years—to go home feeling like failures? If you'd set your goal at $1,300,000, they'd be celebrating enormous success and be ready to sign on for whatever committee work needed to be done next.

Be realistic about defining success when you put numbers to it. Be realistic—but achievable.

And here's where goals *really* become objectives…

4. Is the goal delegated to someone?

If nobody is responsible to accomplish the goal (or each piece of it), it's likely the goal won't be met.

It's not just that people won't jump in and help—for the most part, they will. Especially people who've already joined your team. It's that nobody knows if they're allowed to act on the goal. Will they be stepping on others' toes? Will they discover there's something they didn't know—like that the entire goal had been cancelled last month? And do they have the authority to accomplish the goal? Nobody likes to jump in and do something, only to discover he's wasted his time or she's wasted resources and actually sabotaged a project.

Goals must be connected to real people, who have real authority to act.

5. Does the goal help you fulfill your mission statement?

You may create a wonderful goal that measures up to all four of the previous yardsticks. The goal may generate energy and excitement among members of your task force. But if the goal doesn't help you fulfill your mission, it's distracting you from being who God has called you to be at this time and doing what God has called you to do at this time. You need to set aside that goal and work on goals that *do* help you fulfill your mission.

The Hard Work of Writing Goals and Objectives

Many ministry leaders don't like to write goals and objectives. They think, "You can't measure what we do in ministry; we do good stuff, and you can't put numbers on it."

That sort of thinking leaves goals in some sort of ephemeral world. As long as leaders don't measure what they do, they feel good about it because at least they're accomplishing something—even if they aren't sure how much.

Or they fear that the moment they go public with goals, they'll be held accountable by the board or the pastor.

But if you're going to accomplish something, you need to be bold about goals and objectives. If you state, "We need more volunteers for our program," that's not really an objective, because it's not measurable or specific. Instead, it's more of a wish. And it's a statement that no one can really hold you accountable for. If you recruit just two more volunteers who happen to wander in, you'll reach your "objective" without doing much of anything.

> "Be willing to be held accountable."

Be willing to be held accountable. Think through:

- *Who is going to recruit new volunteers?*
- *How many additional volunteers do we need?*
- *When do we need these volunteers in place?*
- *How will we use them when we get them?*

Getting important things done requires that we be willing to step up and take responsibility—in part by setting goals and objectives.

Maybe you can't accomplish everything right now—or ever. That's why you need to concentrate on goals you can achieve within a set time period. During this process, you also decide what you're *not* going to do.

As you set goals for your ministry, you'll quickly realize that there may be too much for you to reasonably accomplish in the amount of time you have available or with the staff you have on board. You have to pick and choose which goals will give you the best return on your investment of resources (for example, time, staff, energy, budget). You have to decide what goals to not address because you simply can't do them for now.

> **Pick and choose which goals will give you the best return on your investment.**

How Your Core Team Will Operate

Once you've established some goals and objectives, it's time to decide who's going to take responsibility for them. Unless you want to see all the heads in the room turn and look at you (not a good sign), lead a discussion about how your core team is going to operate. That is, will the members of the group do everything, do some things, or simply give sage advice?

Here are some options to consider.

- **Your core team members could divide up the major tasks and ask other church members to help them.**

  Each individual would take responsibility for a different aspect of the work (such as designing ministry descriptions, identifying potential volunteers, and training). This makes the core team a working group rather than just a policy group. This is often a good option for smaller or newer congregations.

- **Your core team might decide it wants to determine program and policy decisions but use existing church committees or ministries to implement the program.**

  For example, the church nominating committee might prepare volunteer position descriptions, and the church board might write the mission statement. Instead of doing the work, the core team will see that it's done effectively. This isn't good news for the person who ends up having to do the actual work of the volunteer ministry.

- **Your core team might decide to focus on the area of greatest need and do nothing else for six months or a year.**

  For example, if no position descriptions exist for volunteers, the core team may want to spend several months just designing position descriptions.

- **Your core team might decide it needs to find a director for the volunteer ministry.**

  This person—whether volunteer or paid—is charged with staffing the program and will organize and administer the details of the ministry. The director is accountable to the core team but might report directly to the senior pastor. The core team can then devote its time to guiding, advising, supporting, and promoting the volunteer program among members of the church.

Note: One of the first things the newly-designated director of the volunteer-equipping ministry should do is find and involve a group of volunteers who will provide active support and help—essentially to function as a core team. If you can recruit a core team that will function in a hands-on fashion, it will make that step unnecessary.

> "Have you made a decision yet about how your core team will function?"

Have you made a decision yet about how your core team will function? If not, make this your top priority, and be sure to create an objective that deals with it!

The Change-Energized Volunteer Ministry

You're about to create some major changes in your church—and that can energize everyone involved. Or not. Here's how to gain permission to move ahead so your ministry thrives.

Some people love change. They're energized by it, and they love the thrill of the unexpected.

Unfortunately, they're in the minority. Most people hate change—at least change initiated by someone else. Unless most people see the need for change, they'll tend to resist it.

If you're going to create a thriving volunteer ministry culture, you need to gain permission for the changes you'll cause. Launching or revitalizing a volunteer ministry may change the way volunteers do their current roles. It will change lines of communication. It will change what's expected of people. It might even change the staff configuration.

The good news is that with some planning and forethought, you can nudge people toward deciding the discomfort they feel is a "growing pain," not another kind of pain.

If you don't do enough planning…well, you may experience what Sue Waechter experienced…

The World's Most Expensive Paperweights

I was the volunteer administrator in a hospital a number of years ago, and we had the opportunity to computerize the reception area so we could retrieve patient information from the hospital's computer system.

The volunteers assigned to the reception area were skeptical about using these machines when the old index card files they'd always used were still functional (and familiar!). In the volunteers' minds, nothing about the way they were doing their work was broken.

So I provided all the reasons we should install computers. It would be so much more state-of-the-art to have computers instead of card files. Information would be more accurate and timely. It would be easier to update information. It would look more professional. The benefits were obvious, at least to me.

I spent weeks selling the idea to the volunteers. They all attended the computer training that I'd arranged for them, and together we awaited the day the computers were installed.

Once the boxes were unpacked, I set up the computers and got them ready for the next day's volunteers. I could hardly wait. When I arrived at work the next morning, I rushed down to the lobby, and there, to my amazement, were two volunteers with the card files at their fingertips—and two computers pushed to the side with a stack of the daily announcements underneath them.

My computers had become the world's most expensive paperweights.

What had gone wrong?

What had gone wrong?

Getting computerized was the culmination of *my* dream, not theirs. I'd sold the idea based on benefits I perceived, but I hadn't identified any benefits *they'd* perceive. All they saw was the need to master a complicated system they hadn't requested, didn't want, and could live without.

Ouch.

I slowed down and started over, spending time helping them discover benefits from their perspective. I allowed them to gradually get more familiar and comfortable with the computers. Eventually, the volunteers came around, and the computers earned a spot on our reception desk.

Was installing computers the right thing for the hospital, and did it meet the needs of the hospital clients? Absolutely. Had I effectively managed the change in the volunteers' eyes? Absolutely not. I didn't consider the losses they would experience—no matter how positive and small the changes seemed to me.

Sometimes changes made in church strike people the same way my changes struck the hospital volunteers. The changes are thrust on people without sufficient time for ending the "way we've always done it" and integrating the new way. People naturally prefer what's familiar, and change represents the unknown.

And your speeches about the benefits from your perspective will fall on deaf ears. Until people discover for *themselves* that making the change is worthwhile, you won't gain permission to lead the charge into bringing about change.

We've observed over the years that congregations seldom respond warmly when someone messes with the "things of faith."

We remember an interim pastor who used a different rhythm when reciting the Lord's Prayer. It so annoyed some of the church members that they griped about it for weeks. The pastor had used the same words. The exact same content. But varying the rhythm was enough to set off a month-long conversation during coffee hour.

How you go about gaining permission to lead change can make or break your volunteer ministry.

How to Gain Permission to Make Changes in Your Church

There are several ways you can help members in the church deal with change and reassure them that it's positive to embrace the change you're proposing.

Most approaches involve face-to-face conversations where you can establish that you're capable of leading the change, establish that you have no ulterior motives, and explain the change clearly. It's also important that you allow enough time for people to discover the good things that will come about as a result of the change and to let go of the past.

Consider these practical suggestions.

1. Help people articulate why things must change.

Del Poling, a consultant who helps churches deal with conflict and change, shared a truly wonderful question with us recently. When Del engages in discussions with a church about change, he begins the process with these questions: *Who are we?* and *Where are we now?*

> "Why can't we stay where we are?"

After the group discusses who they are, what their ministries include, and what their strengths and weaknesses are, he asks them to answer this third question—the wonderful one mentioned earlier—*Why can't we stay where we are?*

What a profound question! It's all well and good for us to describe what we want the future of our congregation to look like. We need to do that. But until we feel the pain of staying in our present situation, we won't be motivated to push ahead into that new, unfamiliar future. As people answer the question, they take on the role of change-agents, suggesting why things should change. They begin to get energized about making a shift, rather than resenting it.

Del told us about a church that asked him to facilitate strategic planning with the church elders. Del knew the church building included a gorgeous parlor, an attractive sanctuary, a welcoming fellowship hall, and a deplorable, run-down Christian education area.

Del asked the person arranging the first meeting to hold it in the Christian education area. When the meeting was scheduled to begin, it was raining, and the meeting attendees sat in an uncomfortable, cramped room where the windows were leaking and wind blew through.

Finally, one leader said, "We can't stay in here any longer!"

That moment presented a memorable opportunity for the group to realize they couldn't stay where they were in how they offered Christian education, either.

This experience was a compelling illustration of what needed to change in that church. Until the leaders experienced the pain of the present, they were not motivated to move into the future.

Some additional questions to ask in regards to your volunteer ministry are:

- *What happens now when church members try to serve as volunteers?*
- *What pain happens in their experience?*
- *If we keep things exactly as they are, what will be the consequences?*
- *In what ways are we failing to live up to our commitment to be disciples of Christ?*
- *What do we need to leave behind if we want to become better disciples of Christ?*

2. Facilitate a dialogue about the coming change.

Remember, for your volunteer ministry to thrive, you've got to help others discover for themselves the benefits of making the changes you know are coming. Your lectures won't do the trick. You've got to get people engaged in dialogue.

Use the same techniques and skills you used to plug church leadership into your ministry. Start by determining who should be involved in the dialogue, who are the invested individuals. Include key decision-makers who have the power to be a barrier to the volunteer ministry either through direct action or by passively not supporting the ministry.

Also include anyone who's expressed an interest in the program and anyone who's expected to carry out program functions. And most *definitely* include people who control resources the program needs, such as money, office space, or equipment. They can starve you out if they don't support the volunteer ministry.

> " And be sure to include those folks we call the 'reed people.' "

Another person to bring on board is the person who'll direct the ministry, if that person has been identified.

And be sure to include those folks we call the "reed people." These people have the power or position to hinder your program. If you fail to include them in the dialogue, they'll hang in the reeds and wait for an opportunity to shoot you out of the water.

3. Help people manage the transitions of change.

In his book *Managing Transitions*, William Bridges describes the stages of change. He writes that it isn't changes that are difficult, it's transitions. "*Change* is not the same as transition. Change is situational: the new site, the new boss, the new team roles, the new policy. *Transition* is the psychological process people go through to come to terms with the new situation. Change is external, transition is internal."

How true! But the good news is that there are three steps you can help people go through that will enable them to transition through change.

- **Say goodbye to the old way.**

    In your case, it's the way your church has always recruited volunteers and how you've always worked together.

You can help people say goodbye by...

Identifying who's losing what. Talk with people to find out what will be hard to let go of. It might be power or a position. It may be that they worked for years with their best friends and now they won't be on the same volunteer teams. They might be required to work in a new place that's more in line with their abilities, skills, and passions. They might even be asked to give up their favorite job!

Validating those losses for individuals. Listen as people talk about the loss they're experiencing, and fully accept that it's painful, no matter how small the loss may seem to you.

Allowing people to grieve openly. Give people permission to talk openly about their sadness or even anger.

Continuing to give people information. In the absence of information, people tend to assume the worst. The more information you can share about what's happening with the volunteer program, the better.

Making the goodbye final. If necessary, tell people the old way will no longer work. Sue had to finally remove the card files from the reception desk in the hospital so they were no longer available to use.

Celebrating the past with respect. Talk about the way things were done with respect. Don't invalidate the past.

- **Transition toward the new way.**

This is the period of time when new things are being introduced and people are still unsure of what's expected. They also wonder what things will look like when everything is in place.

Pray for people to not find the transition too confusing or uncomfortable. It's aggravating to have to deal with change on someone else's schedule, especially when you don't see the need. Ask God to guard the hearts of your volunteers from bitterness or disappointment. Even better—ask God to energize your volunteers for change!

> Ask God to energize your volunteers for change!

Acknowledge that it may be a difficult time. Some people will accept the new approach to volunteer ministry quicker than others. Some people may never accept it. Let people know you understand it may be hard to make the changes.

Redefine this period. The change being experienced isn't watching a ship go down. It's taking a last voyage on one ship and then boarding another—a ship heading toward an exciting destination.

Be clear about processes and procedures. Be specific about how you expect people to do things at this time, even if the processes are temporary.

Keep talking. Create a small team to help facilitate dialogue through the transition, expressing feelings and concerns back to leadership.

- **Begin the new way.**

This is the exciting, energizing initiation of the new way of doing things and working together.

Pray for everyone to see God's vision for the volunteer program at your church, and pray that everyone remains faithful to that vision. The changes you're making aren't random or thoughtless; they're designed to help you more faithfully fulfill God's vision for your program. They're important.

Communicate the big picture and why the volunteer ministry is changing. Do this through newsletters, in meetings, and from the pulpit. Don't rely on one communication channel to reach everyone.

Paint the picture of how it will be when the change is completely integrated into day-to-day life. You can begin to create familiarity with the vision of how things could be.

Ask people what they need during this time. Especially if you see them struggling with new ways of doing things, ask people what information or resources they lack. Be gentle and kind.

Celebrate, and give praise to God for the success of the change.

And here's one last practical idea for encouraging the change process. In a staff meeting or other appropriate gathering, ask people to decide for themselves whether they're just beginning to deal with the change or have already moved through the transition completely.

Ask people to stand somewhere along an imaginary line in the room, with "just beginning to accept and deal with the change" at one wall, and "fully accept the change" at the other wall. Tell people to stand at one extreme or the other, or anywhere in between—whatever spot represents where they are emotionally.

This technique provides an opportunity for people to discuss what barriers or struggles they're experiencing. It also allows people who are further along with the change to provide encouragement to those who are struggling.

The Leadership- Energized Volunteer Ministry

A core team can take you just so far. It's time to put someone in charge…someone who'll keep the volunteer ministry energized and on task.

It's great to have a core team create a vision statement, mission statement, goals, and objectives. Having representatives from each of the volunteer ministry's constituent groups guarantees that you'll design documents that have widespread support and wisdom.

But you *don't* want to have a committee making day-to-day decisions as you implement those goals and objectives. That's a cumbersome process that will slow down decision-making dramatically.

It's not that you never want to reconvene your core team. You may well need one often as the ministry develops and grows. And many of these people may serve as an ongoing board of advisors, if you structure your ministry to include a board. (Hint: Reasons that's wise will be discussed later!)

> It's important you find an equipping ministry champion to run the show.

But for daily decisions? It's important you find an equipping-ministry champion to run the show.

What to Call Your Leader

There are several common titles in use for the person who directs and manages the volunteer process in a church. *Director of equipping ministry* is one common title, as is *connections director*. Some churches communicate the importance of the role by referring to this person as the *pastor of congregational involvement* or another title that prominently includes "pastor."

Pick whatever title works for your church culture and communicates the role clearly, but be aware that first impressions count. There's some wisdom in using the term "pastor" or "minister" in the title if you want to notify the church that volunteer ministry is worthy of respect and attention.

However, for ease, we'll refer to the role as director of equipping ministry for the duration of this chapter.

Responsibilities of the Director of Equipping Ministry

The DEM (Director of Equipping Ministry) may be paid staff or unpaid staff. It may be a full-time or part-time position. In some cases, the position is staffed by several people who have a "job-share" situation.

But however the role is staffed, the basic responsibilities of the DEM remain the same: to identify the ministries that can benefit from volunteer involvement, to invite volunteers into minstry, to promote the volunteer ministry, to interview volunteers, to screen volunteers, to place volunteers in positions, to orient and train volunteers, to ensure supervision for volunteers (defining who volunteers are accountable to), and to evaluate and ensure recognition of volunteers.

That's a *lot* to get accomplished! Small wonder the DEM needs a group of people who'll help!

When you're putting a DEM in place, you need a position description that captures the essential information. *Even if you're the DEM yourself, you need a position description!* It's one way your DEM can stay focused, do what's most important, and be evaluated.

Here's a template for creating a position description for this role.

Title: Director of Equipping Ministry

Position Summary: a paragraph describing the duties and responsibilities of the position

The Strategic Fit: how the volunteer ministry fits into and supports the overall strategy of the church

Key Position Responsibilities: a list of the most common and important job responsibilities (for example, interview all potential volunteers for positions)

Benefits: a list of not only paid benefits, if this is a paid position, but also the more intangible benefits such as the opportunity for growth in human relations skills (Keep in mind that the benefits need to be from the DEM's perspective!)

Qualifications: a list of non-negotiable requirements for the position (for example, is a Christ follower, has a bachelor's degree) and the qualifications that would be nice to have (for example, previous experience as a DEM)

Supervision: who this person is responsible to, who he or she is responsible for, and with whom the DEM is expected to effectively interact

Want to see several sample job descriptions for a director of equipping ministry? See pages 173-176 for two that are currently being used in churches.

Be strategic in selecting a person to lead the volunteer ministry. This individual will play a key role in energizing the volunteers and communicating the vision of the program. A strong leader may not keep a floundering program afloat, but a poor leader will certainly sink it.

> A strong leader may not keep a floundering program afloat, but a poor leader will certainly sink it.

Create the position description before selecting someone to fill the role. It's tempting, if you have someone in mind for the role, to design a description that reflects the skills and experience of that person instead of the position.

Also, take care that the position as described will be respected and understood by your congregation and staff. Here's a story where that didn't happen. Don't let it become your story.

In one church, the "volunteer ministry manager" was recruited (as an unpaid position), given a desk and enough money to create a database, and encouraged to go "do good things." The manager, a member of the church, was nominally introduced to the congregation, but it was never made clear what the vision of the ministry was, nor did the congregation truly understand what this person could and would be doing in the position.

Within a short time, the manager was highly frustrated. Her position had turned into a glorified telephone recruiter for other programs within the church. She was spending her days recruiting individuals to cook for funerals, staff the nursery, and stock the food pantry. This was *not* her vision or what she'd expected!

After a long year, she finally resigned, and her resignation went virtually unnoticed. No one has stepped forward to assume the position since.

If this church *does* find another person for the position, it will have to undo the bad feelings and misunderstandings around the volunteer ministry.

What to Look for in an Equipping-Ministry Champion

Once the position is clearly and explicitly defined, think about who can best do the job. The first person to consider is a champion of the volunteer ministry. Since you're reading this book, this might be you!

Look to see who's served on the core team from the beginning. See who's focused solely on the volunteer ministry. The role will be demanding, so if the person is also singing in the choir, helping in VBS, and organizing the annual rummage sale, you're looking at someone who's too busy.

Here are some general characteristics that are good to see in your director of equipping ministry.

The DEM is typically…

- Able to see potential in anyone and everyone,
- Able to perceive gifts, abilities, skills, and passions,
- A good listener,
- Assertive without being aggressive,
- A good delegator,
- Approachable,
- Comfortable interviewing people,
- A skilled manager,
- Capable of maintaining a computer database (or willing to learn how),
- Someone who knows the congregation, and
- Someone whose enthusiasm and positive regard will *energize* the ministry!

Notice that last characteristic: enthusiasm that will energize the ministry. That's not an afterthought; it's an essential to keep the ministry on track.

Our friend and colleague Marlene Wilson describes herself as an "informed optimist." That means she understands that leaders and volunteers can be petty, caustic, and negative. She knows that sometimes people operate out of less-than-ideal motives. But so what? It's still her job when she's leading volunteers to draw out the best in people. To provide encouragement and vision. To keep everyone on the same page.

We think that's a good place for a volunteer champion to spend time: informed optimism. But not everyone is wired that way.

Being a solid manager is great—but not enough.

Being a good salesperson is great—but not enough.

> It's that blend of positive realism that will energize your ministry from top to bottom, stem to stern.

You need someone who's engaging and a leader. And someone who is determined to be an informed optimist. It's that blend of positive realism that will energize your ministry from top to bottom, stem to stern.

So when you find the right person, how do you bring him or her on board? As a paid staff member or an unpaid volunteer staff member?

To Pay or Not to Pay

Should you pay an equipping-ministry champion? The short answer is: It depends.

Does your congregation have the resources to pay someone to fill this role? If so, you'll have more access to that person. Your DEM won't be fitting in the tasks and responsibilities around a money-making job.

But there's no guarantee that just because you pay someone, that will make the person perform better or that the person will be more reliable or stay in the role longer.

Still—we live in a society that tends to believe we get what we pay for. That is, if it's a paid position, the manager will be perceived as having more power and "pull" than if it's an unpaid position.

So what's the right answer? Again: It depends.

If you, as a church, feel that having a well-organized volunteer ministry is of sufficient value to invest time, energy, space, and prayer into the effort—it's not a stretch to think it's valuable enough to be worth some money, too.

Here are some relevant questions to ask—and answer—as you consider whether to create a paid staff position:

What role in achieving your vision will the volunteer ministry have? How important will it be, given that role, to have someone in that position seen as an equal to other professionals and leaders of ministries?

Do you have the resources to fund the position? If not, can you raise funds for that position? Are you willing to raise the funds?

Do you have individuals with the skills and experience necessary to carry out the position? Will one of them be willing to accept the role as an unpaid staff member?

Some *irrelevant* questions to *not* ask are:

Will the person be more committed if we do/don't pay him or her?

Will the person stay with the position longer if we pay him or her?

Can we still expect a high level of performance from this person if he or she fills the position as an unpaid volunteer staff member?

You don't ask those questions for several reasons:

- **Money doesn't buy commitment; it buys availability.** Paid staff aren't more committed than unpaid volunteers, but they're probably more available. You insult the integrity of volunteers to imply they can be bought. The best ones can't.

- **Nobody can guarantee longevity.** If you pay a DEM, she may move. If you pay her, she may quit. Ditto if you don't pay her.

  > "You insult the integrity of volunteers to imply they can be bought."

  The simple fact is that paychecks don't guarantee longevity—unless someone needs a paycheck and is stepping into the role until a full-time job can be found. In that case alone longevity is likely to be enhanced...but not necessarily.

- **It's a foundational principle that we don't lower standards for volunteers.** If you'd expect a paid staffer to hit a level of excellence, expect an unpaid staff member to hit the same mark.

A colleague discovered that her pastor was growing ever more uncomfortable with her because she was serving in a full-time, unpaid position as a church volunteer manager. He was wondering if he could truly hold her accountable without having a paycheck as leverage. That situation is less about paychecks than the pastor's belief that only money can be a motivator and only paid ministry truly counts.

Your church can pay someone—or not. It's up to you. There are pluses and minuses on both sides of the equation, depending on what resources your church has available.

Some churches begin the volunteer ministry director role as an unpaid position, and eventually they come to value it so highly that it becomes a paid role. Other churches successfully maintain the position as an unpaid staff position.

But either way—it's a staff position. It must have the power and prestige that comes with a true staff position so the person serving as volunteer director can function effectively.

> But either way—it's a staff position.

Make the "paid/unpaid" decision through prayer and discussion, and share with your congregation how that decision was made, and why. And remember: It doesn't pay to cut corners. If you're trying to cut corners by not paying someone, where else are you cutting corners? Will you provide the funds, support, and involvement the volunteer ministry needs to be viable?

Two Ways to Support Your Equipping-Ministry Champion

First, ensure that the DEM is directly responsible to the senior pastor or an associate pastor.

Whether the person responsible for leading your volunteer ministry is an unpaid volunteer or a paid staff member, the director of equipping ministry should be considered *at the same level as any other ministry director in your church.*

In other words, the DEM is just as important as your music and worship director, your youth director, or your director of Christian education. Your DEM needs to be on the same routing slips as other leaders and sit in the same staff planning sessions.

The volunteer ministry exists to support every other area of ministry by inviting people to fill key positions. Volunteer ministry directors need to know what's going on, which ministry areas are expanding or shrinking, and what upcoming needs might be.

A second way to ensure support and nurture for your DEM is to establish an advisory team or board. This team will provide continuous feedback and input to the ministry. As already mentioned, it can be composed of...

• Representatives from the original core team,

• Program or ministry leaders from within the church,

• Other church staff members, and

• Active volunteers in the church.

Just like your original core team, the advisory team will be chartered and given job descriptions. Approach forming an advisory team the same way you approached forming a core team.

This team can meet periodically to give input, assess the volunteer ministry, and continue to uplift the ministry in prayer. In addition, this team can serve as ambassadors for the volunteer ministry throughout the church and into the community.

A well-chosen team is worth its weight in gold. Work with your DEM to create one. The right blend of people will energize your energizer and keep him or her mindful of all the good that's being accomplished through the volunteer ministry.

> A well-chosen team is worth its weight in gold.

In ministry, like life, little happens without energy. But energy isn't a bottomless well; without help your reserve of enthusiasm and energy will eventually be used up.

That's why you need for your ministry to be energized by more than you. You can do—and *are* doing—tremendous things. But you can't do *everything*, so you need to plug yourself and the volunteer ministry into the life-giving energy of...

People—both the church leadership and church membership

Vision—one that inspires, defines the program, and attracts volunteers

Mission—that provides clear purpose

Prayer—personal and corporate time with God that refreshes your heart and renews your perspective, humor, and perseverance

The energy sizzling from these sources will empower your goals, invigorate your core team, and fortify your spirit as you continue to charge full speed ahead toward the future God has in mind for your church and your ministry.

Ready to go the distance? We know you are, but first we want to offer you some wise words of encouragement.

Wise Words and Encouragement— for You

We close this book with some wisdom, insights, and inspiration.

This challenge got us thinking about the concept of wisdom and led us to revisit some favorite quotes from T. S. Eliot:

"Where is the life we have lost in living?

"Where is the wisdom we have lost in knowledge?

"Where is the knowledge we have lost in information?"

–T.S. Eliot, *The Complete Poems and Plays 1909-1950*. Copyright 1971 by Esme Valerie Eliot (New York: Harcourt, Brace & World, Inc.), p.96.

Pondering the idea of wisdom and reflecting on this quote, here are the things we believe about wisdom:

- Wisdom deals with the "why" questions; knowledge and information deal with the "what and how."

- Wisdom deals with future implications; knowledge and information tend to concentrate on the present.

- Wisdom deals with principles and values (paradigms); knowledge and information deal with practices.

- Wisdom seeks to understand the questions; knowledge and information look for the answers.

- Wisdom is going deeper; knowledge and information tend to just keep getting broader.

Wisdom deals with the "whys" of what we do, with the future implications of our decisions, and with the principles and values underlying our decisions and practices. Wisdom calls us to be willing to ask hard questions that move us deeper into the meaning of what we do.

It's not that knowledge and information aren't important! They're essential in helping us reshape, re-form, and innovate our practices in the field of volunteer leadership. Knowledge and information keep us viable and appropriate.

But there is an intriguing tension between knowledge/information and wisdom. It is often the challenge of what to let go of—and what to hold fast to—in the midst of all the changes. As T. S. Eliot also said:

> "We shall not cease from exploration, and the end of all exploring will be to arrive where we started—and know the place for the first time."
>
> –T.S. Eliot, *The Complete Poems and Plays 1909-1950*, p.145.

We've summarized some powerful principles that have stood the test of time through our collaborative efforts in leading volunteers in the church and nonprofit setting. They're what we still believe, after all this time, about leadership, management, volunteerism, and groups.

We share these principles with you, knowing that the real value isn't what we're writing here. Rather, we hope it will encourage you to make your own list!

Powerful Principles to Go the Distance in Volunteer Leadership

1. Volunteers are priceless.

We can sum up this belief in a simple line we heard more than 30 years ago: *Volunteers are not paid—not because they're worthless, but because they're priceless!*

Contrast that attitude toward volunteers with others you may have witnessed:

"Volunteers are nice, but not necessary."

"Volunteers are more work than they're worth."

"They're okay, as long as they don't cost us anything."

"We'll use them to save money, but they should be seen and not heard."

The attitudes of your church leadership toward volunteers permeates your church and has a dramatic effect on how volunteers feel about serving there. We believe in volunteers. We urge you to do the same.

2. People must be as important as programs, products, or profits.

The truth is that leaders either grow or diminish those who work with them. So if we meet our goals at the expense of the health, well-being, and growth of our people, we've ultimately failed. Everything we do in a volunteer-equipping process must be grounded in these basics of theology:

- The priesthood of all believers
- The whole body of Christ
- The giftedness of each child of God

We haven't always embraced these theologies. For example, in the 1950s, many churches focused on creating excellent programs. We decided to only let those who were excellent singers sing…only the excellent musicians could play during worship services…and we lost people who weren't professional performers.

In the 1990s, corporations focused so much on products and profits that they sometimes worked people literally to death—at least the death of their marriages.

People are important, too. They're designed for eternity.

3. People become committed to plans they help make. So plan *with*, not *for*, people.

This idea has gone through several fads and phases over the years, such as "participative management" and "quality circles." Organizations spent millions bringing in gurus to teach them how to do planning...but many organizations never caught *why* planning *with* people makes sense.

It makes sense because the real wisdom is in the team itself. That's where the corporate genius resides, as well as the motivation to see plans succeed.

 Far too often it became a gimmick to manipulate groups, and that always failed. People are too smart for this!

Stephen Covey, in his book *The 7 Habits of Highly Effective People*, observed, "It simply makes no difference how good the rhetoric is, or even how good the intentions are. If there is little or no trust, there is no foundation for permanent success. Only basic goodness gives life to techniques."

4. Mission motivates; maintenance does not.

That's why one of your primary tasks is casting the vision, then keeping it alive.

Vision must be tied to tasks—that provides action.

Action must be tied to vision—that provides purpose and meaning.

Vision alone isn't enough. Action alone isn't enough.

Make sure everyone who works with you—volunteers and staff—knows your mission and how their work makes it happen.

5. Integrity and trust are the leader's most powerful assets; they have to be carefully and patiently earned.

If this is true, then the foundation for all team building is three-pronged: truth, trust, and clear expectations.

6. You must care for and tend your teams.

As go your teams, so goes your ministry. Watch carefully so you know how a team is developing. You may see…

A *parasitic* team (competitive) where 1 + 1 = less than two.

A *symbiotic* team (cooperative) where 1 + 1 = 2.

A *synergistic* team (collaborative) where 1 + 1 = 3.

Grow healthy teams that move toward synergy. It's so simple—but so often overlooked because of expediency.

7. Avoid the trap of becoming either a specialist or a generalist.

A specialist is someone who knows more and more about less and less, until they know practically everything about almost nothing. A generalist is someone who knows less and less about more and more until they know almost nothing about everything.

8. Be yourself—no one else is better qualified.

In other words, be true to your principles and not swayed by fad or fashion. There is no substitute for being congruent in what you say and what you do—it builds trust in others and gives you peace of mind. For example, be sure to work with volunteer teams yourself. It's what gives you credibility and makes you an effective advocate for team ministry.

9. The key to wise leadership is effective delegation, and the key to delegation (and motivation) is finding the right people for the right ministries.

Do not only accept but actually seek out someone who knows more than you do where you need help. Then let them do the job—and be glad they succeed!

How do you get the right people in the right positions? Know them by talking to them (interviewing) and observing them in action. Watch when their eyes light up. McClelland's Theory of Motivation of achievers, affiliators, and power people can be incredibly helpful to you for this concept.

10. Motivating others is critical to your success.

I believe what John Gardner, in his book *On Leadership*, said about motivation: "Leaders do not create motivation...they unlock or channel existing motives."

Let your own enthusiasm, excitement, and dedication to your mission shine through your work—it's contagious!

11. To become advocates and innovators, develop these three C's in your life: curiosity, creativity, and courage.

With those qualities in your life, be alert to identify problems and challenges that "have your name on them" (because of your past experience and skill), and take ownership of them.

Don't worry about knowing how to solve the problems; figuring it out is the fun part. And you don't need to know how it will all turn out. Just step up to the plate and take on issues when it's time to engage; let go when it's time to let go.

12. You can't help others if you don't stay well yourself. So take care of you!

In this world it's often a great challenge to survive. But plants survive. Dogs and cats survive. I want to live embracing life with empathy and a zeal born out of passion. That's living...and that's the goal.

We've heard it said that each of us is a house with four rooms—physical, mental, emotional, and spiritual. Most of us tend to live in one room most of the time. But unless we go into every room every day, even if only to keep it aired out, we're not complete people. What a vivid metaphor for health and wholeness!

If you're serious about staying well, you will find time to:

- **Do the necessary housecleaning to rid your rooms of clutter and toxic waste.** This means "letting go" of lots of stuff! (You can't stumble on things that are behind you.)

- **Know your own needs**. If you can't name your own needs, then you don't deserve to have them met.

- **Be sure to not only visit each of your rooms every day but slowly and lovingly furnish those rooms with things that nourish you, replenish you, and give you joy.** No one can do that for you. We need to be the caretakers of our own lives.

13. It's important to keep the soul in our work.

Wayne Muller, in his book *Sabbath: Restoring the Sacred Rythym of Rest*, tells the story of a South American tribe that would go on long marches day after day. All of a sudden they would stop walking, sit down, rest, and then make camp for a couple of days. They explained that they needed the time to rest so their souls could catch up with them. A concept to love.

Our hope for you is that you'll rise to the challenges in volunteer leadership with clear vision, a list of your own powerful principles, new and creative "how to's," and all the energy, enthusiasm, dedication, joy—and yes, *soul*—you have! That you have the wisdom to determine what to keep, what to change, what to drop—and what to create.

To do this you'll need the courage of pioneers, the ingenuity of entrepreneurs, the enthusiasm and fearlessness of 5-year-olds, the dedication and compassion of volunteers, and the wisdom of Solomon.

One final thing: You'll need the firm faith that nothing worthwhile is ever impossible with God's help.

Sample Forms for Volunteer Leadership

Adapt any of the forms you find here. They're yours for the taking, as long as you use them in your local church setting. Keep in mind that no form or position description is truly a "one-size-fits-all" solution, so give serious thought to personalizing these items for your unique situation. Make sure they reflect your church's values, culture, and personality.

- Core Team Charter Covenant
- Core Team Member Position Description
- Volunteer Ministry Vision and Mission Statements
- Creating Vision and Mission Statements
- Director of Equipping Ministry Sample Position Descriptions

Core Team Charter Covenant—Sample

Core Team Name: Volunteer Ministry Core Team

Core Team Mission *(Purpose)***:**

Our mission is to explore the scope and possibilities that God intends for an organized volunteer ministry for our church.

Core Team Vision *(Desired outcomes)***:**

When our work is done, we will clearly understand what God calls us to build in the volunteer ministry, and we will have laid the foundation for that ministry.

Core Team Sponsor:

Church board

The Sponsor's Role:

Two board members will sit on the core team.

Core Team Authority:

This core team can pray and discern what God intends for the volunteer ministry. This core team can engage the congregation to determine what their needs are in a volunteer ministry. This core team can recommend to the board the elements necessary for a viable volunteer ministry, including staff, support, space, and financial resources.

This core team cannot—without approval—spend more than $500 on research or materials.

Core Team Member Roles and Responsibilities *(What tasks will be accomplished, and by whom—that is, who will call the meetings, who will facilitate the meetings)*:

- Maria will create and send out the agendas and facilitate the meetings.
- Tom will arrange for the meeting rooms and equipment needed.
- José will remind members of refreshment sign-ups.
- Ruth will type meeting notes and distribute via e-mail.
- Devotions will be shared, and members will sign up for meetings.
- Victor will write articles for the newsletter and announcements.

Core Team Time Frame:

This core team will have completed its work when the foundation for the volunteer ministry is complete and others are designated to manage the ministry. This core team may be available for a period to offer support to those who are designated.

Core Team Decision-Making *(How decisions will be made)*:

We will make decisions by consensus, with a fallback of a vote with a simple majority. (We define consensus as a decision that everyone can "live with" and actively support.)

Core Team Interactions *(Ground rules)*:

- We will always do full devotions at the beginning of our meetings.
- We will always end our meetings with prayer.
- We will speak one at a time and listen carefully to each other.
- We will check out assumptions before we leap to conclusions.
- We will affirm each other for the work we are doing together.
- We will start our meetings on time and end on time.

Core Team Interface With Others *(How this core team will communicate with others)*:

We will list who we need to communicate with at the end of each meeting to ensure that we are communicating the right amount of information to the right people in the right way.

Core Team Progress:

- We will set specific goals and measure progress on those goals at each meeting.
- We will assess involvement of other stakeholders.

Core Team Feedback *(How to get feedback on what the team is doing)*:

- We will ask for feedback when we are interacting with other groups and individuals in the church.
- We will acknowledge the support we get from others through prayer and assistance.

Core Team Celebration:

- We will acknowledge our own achievements on our goals.
- We will celebrate as we move forward toward our vision.
- We will celebrate our work together when we sunset.

Core Team Member Position Description

Position Summary: The Volunteer Ministry Core Team exists to explore the scope and possibilities that God intends for an organized volunteer ministry for [name of church]. Members of the core team will be committed to prayer and discernment to this end. Members will work together to assess needs of the congregation and opportunities for an organized volunteer ministry.

The core team will also assist in implementing programming to meet those needs through the creation of a volunteer-equipping ministry.

The Strategic Fit: We're called to provide nurture and care to each other as Christians. We're also called to be good stewards of the resources given to us by God. An effective and efficient volunteer ministry will help our church do and be both. Our church's vision is [fill in].

Key Responsibilities:

- To pray unceasingly for the volunteer ministry.

- To attend meetings to determine the scope of the volunteer ministry.

- To do work outside of meetings when requested to assess the congregation's needs.

- To assume tasks that will establish the volunteer ministry. These tasks may include creating position descriptions, interviewing potential volunteers, or other tasks that will help establish the volunteer ministry.

- To follow through with people and activities to achieve the goals of the core team.

- To communicate the work of the core team with others openly and honestly.

Benefits: Being a member on the core team will provide…

- The opportunity to interact with other believers in the congregation.
- The chance to grow spiritually through discipline of focused prayer, reading of Scripture, and devotions.
- An opportunity to impact this ministry from the beginning.
- The opportunity to be a significant contributor to the church's vision.

Qualifications:

- It would be helpful if the core team member had some experience with this congregation.
- It will be important that the core team member has the ability and willingness to commit and follow through.
- It would be helpful if the core team member has been a volunteer within the church before.

Supervision: The core team member is responsible to the core team chair and/or the sponsor of the core team. The core team member is also responsible to honor the ground rules of the core team.

Signature(s) of Core Team Member(s) _____

Date _____

(Note: You can have individual members sign a charter, or do it as a group.)

Volunteer Ministry Vision and Mission Statements—Samples

3 Sample Vision Statements

We will be a volunteer community that:

- Attracts people,
- Creates a volunteer experience that enables the discovery and sharing of spiritual gifts,
- Keeps volunteers connected and interested, and
- Meets the people's needs of the church's identified programs.

Our vision is to guarantee that every volunteer is empowered, equipped to use his or her gifts, valued, trained, utilized, and appreciated.

We will increasingly become a uniquely compassionate community reflecting Christ's presence by actively serving others, actively receiving and sharing God's Word of Law and gospel, and actively lifting up prayer as the heartbeat for our daily living and for the daily life of our church.

3 Sample Mission Statements

The Volunteer Ministry exists to show God's love by giving of ourselves to meet the many needs of Living Hope Baptist Church.

> (Living Hope Baptist Church, Bowling Green, Kentucky)

The Volunteer Services Ministry at Southeast exists to make it easy for people to connect with God, the church, and one another through volunteer service to Christ.

> (Southeast Christian Church, Louisville, Kentucky)

Helping people in need and following Christ's command that we love one another lies at the heart of our Christian faith.

> (Bedford Presbyterian Church, Bedford, New York)

Creating Vision and Mission Statements

Steps for Creating a Mission Statement Worksheet

1. Whom do we serve?

_____

_____

2. What services do we provide?

_____

_____

3. What's unique about us within this church?

_____

_____

Now craft a simple statement:

What's the most important phrase from everything you wrote above? (*It goes first.*)

Then follow this first phrase with the remaining phrases.

_____

_____

_____

After you have a statement, review it again, and see if you can cut out any text. You want to be as brief and clear as possible. Simplify where you can.

Director of Equipping Ministry
Position Descriptions — Samples

Sample 1

Position Description

Membership Ministries Coordinator
First Presbyterian Church of Granville, Ohio

Position Summary

The Membership Ministries Coordinator helps members and friends of the church identify and claim their gifts, talents, and areas of interest for personal growth and helps them identify areas of ministry. The Membership Ministries Coordinator identifies and profiles needs of the church and its ministry, both within the congregation and outside of the church in mission areas.

Purpose of the Position

An important but often neglected spiritual ministry of the church is to call forth, name, and encourage the use of the gifts of members. These gifts have their source in God and are best expressed in some form of Christian service. The Membership Ministries Coordinator takes the lead in coordinating this ministry of gifts and assisting members and friends in linking their interests and abilities with the needs of the church and the world.

Authority

The Membership Ministries Coordinator is a member of the staff, attending one staff meeting per month, and reports to the pastor who has responsibility for membership.

Responsibilities

- Develop goals, actions, and budget at least annually.

- Develop, or supervise the development of, position descriptions for volunteer roles.

- Regularly interview and assist members and friends of the church to identify their gifts and talents, areas for personal growth, and their sense of calling.

- Maintain a current database containing this information. Assist with their integration into service.

- Maintain support systems for volunteers: placement, training, supervision, feedback, and recognition.

- Regularly profile the needs of the church, both within the congregation and outside of the church in its areas of mission. Maintain a current database containing this information.

- Assist church leaders as they invite volunteers to serve in ministry.

- Communicate regularly throughout the congregation to keep members and friends informed.

- Keep current on congregational events, issues, initiatives, opportunities, and challenges.

Qualifications for Position

The Membership Ministries Coordinator will possess management skills, will know the congregation, will work well with a variety of people, will be present during worship on Sunday, and will be motivated by the creative possibilities within the life of the congregation.

Terms of the Position

The duties and performance within this position will be reviewed annually by the head of staff. The position requires 10 hours per week and is a volunteer position.

Sample 2

Position Description

Title: Coordinator of Volunteer Ministry

Department: Outreach Ministries

Reports To: Associate Pastor of Outreach Ministries

Objective

To increase and maximize the number of volunteer opportunities and match more members to those opportunities. To promote spiritual growth by the concept that each person is serving in ministry when they respond to their faith as members of Christ's church (that is, priesthood of all believers, whole body of Christ, and giftedness of each child of God).

Specific Responsibilities/Duties

- Design and implement volunteer invitation strategies to encourage more involvement from the congregation.

- Develop, or supervise the development of, position descriptions for volunteer roles.

- Design and implement volunteer retention strategies.

- Develop and maintain appropriate systems (such as one-on-one interviews) to help match members' gifts, talents, and abilities to appropriate and meaningful ministry opportunities.

- Develop procedures to involve the members in ministry opportunities, and follow up on placements of volunteers.

- Develop and maintain up-to-date records concerning volunteer services within the congregation.

- Present information about the volunteer ministry at all new-member classes.

- Serve as a resource person to church staff and lay leaders:

   Help them work with volunteers in designing strategies for the recruitment and retention of volunteers for their respective ministries;

   Help them initiate training for volunteers as needed; and

   When necessary (and subject to the approval of the Associate Pastor of Outreach Ministries), personally contact church members to recruit them as volunteers.

- Facilitate recognition and appreciation for volunteers in ongoing and meaningful ways.

- Participate as a team member of staff, including attending staff meetings and regularly attending worship services at [church name].

- Be available for other assignments and projects as needed and assigned.

Qualifications:

Faith/Spiritual Life: Committed Christian, with a strong Christian faith. Maintains a Christian lifestyle and active devotional life. Actively demonstrates Christian faith through lifestyle and actions.

Abilities/Skills: Good planning and organizational skills. Good communication skills, both written and verbal. Demonstrates strong teamwork and strong interpersonal skills. Goal-oriented and resourceful. Good knowledge of self and personal and spiritual gifts.

Education/Training: B.A. in education or related field preferred. Training or experience in volunteer ministries or recruiting volunteers preferred. Experience working with and directing people. Experience working as a volunteer. Experience working with a variety of computer programs.